"Kyle Searcy personifies wisdom. From parenting to pastoring, Kyle fuses the wisdom of Solomon with the compassion of the Good Samaritan and the evangelistic passion of Peter at Pentecost. His biblical and practical insights on wisdom contain the potential to radically improve all features of your life!"

Dr. Jay Wolf, pastor, First Baptist Church, Montgomery, Alabama

"Life is composed of choices. The quality of wisdom is choice. Kyle Searcy offers biblical, practical, theologically significant insights into how to select biblical wisdom rather than human or secular wisdom. His teaching comes out of his own faith journey. Choosing biblical wisdom puts us on the path of fulfilling God's purpose."

Dr. John Ed Mathison, John Ed Mathison Leadership Ministries; Frazer United Methodist Church

"We can get enough food, water and other essentials of life, but one can never have enough wisdom. Accessing wisdom from within and without is a constant quest for those who seek to grow and help others do the same. In *The Secrets of Biblical Wisdom*, Pastor Kyle Searcy will lead you on a journey of acquiring wisdom while removing all the mystique. I want to be wiser. Don't you?"

Dr. Samuel R. Chand, author, *Cracking Your Church's Culture Code*; www.samchand.com

"Kyle Searcy is a leadership expert whom people should be following, and his book *The Secrets of Biblical Wisdom* is a good reason. Leadership is built on strong decisions, and wisdom is a powerful foundation. Get this book. It's never too late to be reminded of the power of wise choices."

Phil Cooke, filmmaker and media consultant; author, *One Big Thing: Discovering What You Were Born to Do*

THE SECRETS OF
BIBLICAL
*W*ISDOM

THE SECRETS OF
BIBLICAL
WISDOM

Unleashing the Power of
Heavenly Insight in Your Life

KYLE SEARCY

Chosen

a division of Baker Publishing Group
Minneapolis, Minnesota

© 2012 by Kyle C. Searcy

Published by Chosen Books
11400 Hampshire Avenue South
Bloomington, Minnesota 55438
www.chosenbooks.com

Chosen Books is a division of
Baker Publishing Group, Grand Rapids, Michigan

Printed in the United States of America

Library of Congress Cataloging-in-Publication Data is available for this title.

ISBN 978-0-8007-9534-4

Note that all names in the stories included in the text have been changed to protect individual privacy.

Cover design by Kirk DouPonce, DogEared Design

12   13   14   15   16   17   18   7   6   5   4   3   2

Contents

Foreword

It was half time. We were losing a game to a lesser rival, and it was both frustrating and embarrassing to all of us. Our college football coach, the late Robert Odell (a Heisman Trophy runner-up), gave a speech that challenged my young teammates and me to the core. He said with a gruff resolve that could never be imitated, "Potential is interesting but performance is everything." He was telling us that we outclassed our opponents in every way, except the way that counted that afternoon. His words were like goads that pricked our consciences.

The coach's speech had tapped into a visceral level of wisdom. His wisdom inspired us collectively to rise against a seemingly insurmountable challenge (given the flawed first half). His words empowered our entire team to think and act differently. And in response to his chiding, we did what we knew how to do and won the game.

What is wisdom? Among a myriad of other things, it is the art of taking facts or nasty realities and turning these raw materials into competent action, solved problems, healed relationships or fulfilled dreams. Wisdom is a game winner. Everyone thinks they have it. Yet like common sense, it is uncommon.

Wisdom is the answer to our greatest military problems, our world-wide economic woes and important situations too numerous to count. One hundred percent wisdom is impossible to attain, so who could dare write a book on wisdom? Someone who knows that wisdom is not a destination at the end of a winding road but rather a refreshing substance passed on to us like water to a weary desert traveler. At best, the wisest of us has extraordinary communion with someone who passes on to us this life-sustaining gift.

Kyle Searcy is a fellow traveler who speaks only about the kinds of roads he has traveled. He speaks only from what he has learned by viewing life through the lenses of biblical truth. He speaks only what he has learned through trial and error. In real sense, Kyle has not just given us nuggets of wisdom but has shared with us "a way of wisdom." This is all made possible because he has found a way of accessing wisdom from our Source—Jesus. Kyle has given us incredible stories and prayers that will bring serve as water to thirsty readers reaching toward new dimensions of wisdom.

Kyle has also made *The Secrets of Biblical Wisdom* a fun and exciting read. Please remember that this work is more than just a handbook for every Christian, regardless of your time in the Kingdom. It is a resource that fosters a relationship with the Lord that is real and practical and has the potential to change your life! The question is whether you will hear the words of my coach from years ago—"Potential is interesting but performance is everything!"

I hope you will choose action, performance and fruitfulness. Then after you have read Kyle's words, continue the miracle. Give this book to your most valued friends.

Bishop Harry R. Jackson Jr.
Senior pastor of the Hope Connection in the
Washington, D.C., and Orlando, FL, areas
Presiding bishop of the International Communion of
Evangelical Churches

Prologue

Several years ago my daughter Hannah had a fascinating dream in which her mother and I were dropping her off at college. When given her room assignment, she was told it was in a particular building on the "Gray Floor." "What do you think that means?" Hannah asked when relating the dream to me.

I knew from a study I had been doing that in the Scriptures the color gray symbolized wisdom—*gray hair* and *elder* actually come from the same word. "In your school, a place that represents learning, you were assigned to live on the floor of Wisdom," I told her.

Then she said, "Dad, when they gave me my room it was number 601. I know that seems strange, but it was very clear in my dream—601."

Instantly I knew what this meant, also. With my love of word studies, I had examined the Greek words *reveal* and *revelation* enough to remember their numbers in Strong's numbering system for New Testament words: 601 and 602.

"You were assigned the room of Revelation on the floor of Wisdom," I told her. Immediately I was reminded of Ephesians 1:17, "That the God of our Lord Jesus Christ, the Father of glory, may give to you a spirit of wisdom and of revelation in the knowledge of Him" (NASB).

Hannah's dream launched me on a quest to better understand the inter-workings of these two aspects of learning. The symbolic designations of her room (Revelation) and floor (Wisdom) were intriguing. Wisdom was broader and provided something to build on, yet it wasn't complete without a room of Revelation. Neither would be adequate or functional without the other. Revelation—that which is revealed to us by the Holy Spirit concerning a particular matter or subject—must be interpreted in the larger context of wisdom—a general understanding of God's ways, purposes and principles learned over time. *Every floor of Wisdom must have a room of Revelation,* I realized, *and every room of Revelation must be found on the floor of Wisdom.*

In *The Secrets of Biblical Wisdom*, my dear friend Kyle Searcy has found the dormitory in Hannah's dream. Laced with revelation, his clear insights on wisdom come alive. In them I found not only understanding but also relevance. He shared more than the *what* with me, but also the *why* and the *how*. Sometimes I read or listen to brilliance and find myself asking, "Who cares?" But as I read this book, I found Kyle's brilliance—and make no mistake about it, he is brilliant—flowing off the pages and into my "applicable" file on a regular basis. I knew I could apply his wisdom; I could build with his insights. You'll have the same experience.

You are holding in your hands a treasure map, my friend. Follow it and you'll discover great enrichment; apply its principles and you'll find success. Life is far too precious to waste; make sure you live it wisely!

Dutch Sheets
Executive Director, Christ for the Nations Institute
Author, *Authority in Prayer* and *Intercessory Prayer*

Acknowledgments

I want to thank Jesus, Jan Sherman, Jane Campbell and the Chosen staff. I also want to thank Bishop Harry Jackson for his encouragement and for connecting me with Chosen. I want to express deep appreciation to my wife, Kemi, our family and the church family I dearly love.

Introduction

I recently returned from a trip that was one of the most favorable and fruitful I have ever taken. I went to Ghana, West Africa, to take part in the *Fresh Fire* conference at Word Miracle Church International. Bishop Charles Agyinasare was the conference host, and Dr. Morris Cerullo was one of the keynote speakers, along with me. The entire experience was life changing. Not only was the conference laced with the fire and glory of God, but my personal times with the Lord were also life transforming. I came back to America with new insight, new grace and a new focus, and of course, I also received *fresh fire*.

I returned home extremely excited. I could not wait to preach that next Sunday. I just knew the Lord would lead me to teach a message on fresh fire, fresh Holy Spirit or fresh something. Whatever it was, I was certain He would want me to release what I received while I was in Africa. I quieted myself before the Lord and began to ask Him, "What should I share?"

As I waited on the Lord, He strongly directed my mind toward the topic of wisdom. Since wisdom had little to do with the words *fresh* or *fire*, I hesitated for a moment. I continued to incline my heart toward heavenly insight, but the impression did not change. Scriptures on wisdom and its importance in our lives flooded my mind. I became convinced that the living God was directing me to concentrate on this essential subject.

The moment the Lord instructed me to share on wisdom, I knew instinctively that it was one of the most important things to focus on for the days ahead. I felt how urgent and important it is for God's people to begin embracing wisdom as a leading grace in their lives. I knew God was ready to release it to His people in much greater measures. I also understood that as a condition of receiving wisdom, we must value its wealth, submit to its operation and pursue its impartation.

Immediately I launched on a pursuit of wisdom that continues to this day. I must have more wisdom. I desire it deeply. I long for it earnestly and pursue it persistently. Wisdom has power to transform our lives and shape our future.

Throughout this book, I will share what wisdom is and what it does. My aim is not theological understanding alone. I seek to create in you an insatiable thirst for wisdom. I want you hungry for it. I want wisdom to become your primary pursuit. I want to seek and find it together with you so that we may reap the fruit of its sweet reward. As we unlock the secrets of biblical wisdom together, our lives will change for the better.

Read on . . . wisdom awaits!

1

When Do You Know
It's the Real Thing?

I knew this would be one of the most important decisions of my life. Having dated many girls since my early teens, I thought finding a wife would be easy. I would just pick the one whom I liked and woo her until I won her. But now, things were different. I was newly born-again, so God had entered the marriage equation.

To complicate matters, I had decided to go into the ministry. I was in my early twenties and felt the time was ripe for marriage, but I had to choose wisely—not everyone could handle the role of a pastor's wife. Destiny hung over my head, weighing on my decision. I did not want anything to alter the call God had on my life. The impact of my choice called for me to sort things out.

I took long walks in the park and considered the kind of woman who might fit into my new life. I would need her to love God—a lot! I would need her to embrace who I was as a person and what I was planning to do with my life. Beyond my needs, I have to admit that I had some desires. Would she be pretty? How would she dress? Then, there beckoned the awkward question of how a future pastor dates someone. Should we only talk about spiritual matters . . . or could we just be like everyone else and discover who we were as people? For the next four and a half years, I spent much time pondering such questions. Somehow, I knew this preparation was grooming me to select just the right girl.

I sought for some measure of how I should go about the process of finding a life partner. I scoured the Scriptures that held principles about choosing a mate. I read stories about how God directed people toward marriage. One evening I read Genesis 24, and the words began jumping off the page. In this passage, we find Abraham had grown too old to search for a wife for his beloved son, Isaac. To keep his son from marrying into the heathen populace around them, Abraham made his servant promise to find Isaac a wife from their own family back in the "old country." The servant was uncertain what he should do if such a girl refused to travel back with him to meet Isaac. Abraham assured him that if the woman did not wish to come to their land, the servant would be released from his duty.

The servant traveled back to Abraham's homeland, sat by a well and saw a group of young ladies approach to fetch water. He asked the Lord,

> "May it be that when I say to a girl, 'Please let down your jar that I may have a drink,' and she says, 'Drink, and I'll water your camels too'—let her be the one you have chosen for your servant Isaac. By this I will know that you have shown kindness to my master."
>
> Genesis 24:14

One girl did stop and offer water for both the servant and his camels. This young woman, Rebekah, just happened to be related to Abraham. She seemed like an answer to prayer, but the final test would come when Abraham's servant met her father and set the bride-price. Would Rebekah be willing to leave her family, travel to an unknown land and become the wife of an unknown man? She was! She simply said, "I will go" (verse 58).

This amazing story became a guiding light for my search. I wanted God to show me in a similar manner whom He wanted me to marry (no camels needed). And the true test would be when she said yes.

My search began. I became friends with a number of lovely young women to whom I was attracted and who were doing their own searching for just the right mate. It started with Sally, the first lady my eyes saw at the campus Bible study I joined. (Names have been changed throughout my stories to protect individual privacy.) She was slim and pretty, and she had a godly demeanor that I respected. To top it all off, she had a gift of singing. I could see us ministering together; her voice would perfectly complement my preaching! She seemed a bit quiet and shy, which appealed to me for some reason.

The second possibility was a young lady named Lydia. Our senior pastor had partnered us to lead the college ministry in our church. I admired Lydia because of her great intellect. She was stately and tall. I could not help imagining, even though I knew it was shallow to think this way, that we really looked great together. Our styles and appearance were similar. Not only that, but she had a soft, kind heart and was compassionate toward people. I loved these traits. Many of our college friends automatically assumed Lydia would become my wife. Marrying her seemed like the logical thing to do.

Then I met Marian. She came highly recommended by an older couple who thought she would be perfect for me. Marian displayed godly traits and was a very serious person. I respected Mr. and Mrs. Phelps, whom I saw as my spiritual parents, and I felt I needed to consider their advice seriously. I felt I should give special weight to their thoughts about my future with Marian.

Another young lady named Cindy was very attentive. She did all she could to dote on me. She would ask if I had eaten or was getting enough rest. If I needed anything, I knew Cindy would drop everything and meet my request if she could. This kind of treatment can be flattering and spoil the little boy in every man.

These were a few of the lovely young women from whom I might choose a wife. What should I do? Who was the right one? If you had been there to advise me, what would you have said? Would you have picked Sally, Lydia, Marian or Cindy? Or would you have shown me a guiding spiritual principle by which I could make my own decision?

I will fill you in on my decision in a minute. But first, I want to discuss making right choices, which is an integral part of exercising supernatural wisdom. Supernatural wisdom is available to every Christian, and I hope this book will help you discover not only how to become wiser, but how to share in the benefits wisdom can bring to your life on a daily basis. Right choices are just one of those benefits.

Wisdom Always Gets It Right

Every human being has weighty decisions to make at one time or another. For you it may not involve whom to marry, but the particular decision you face may impact your life on just as grand a scale. What if you received a money-back guarantee that right answers were available whenever you needed them? Who would not jump at such a fantastic deal? Don't you wish sometimes you could plug your brain into the most technologically advanced database and get the best answers to pressing problems? Have you ever thought about how cool it would be if you could, just like Neo in *The Matrix*, call the Controller and request that a program be downloaded in your brain to enable you to do things proficiently that you normally are not equipped or trained to do?

Have you ever wished you could hire a staff of seasoned advisors to help you make brilliant decisions and correct choices? Think about the convenience of having Dr. Phil or an equivalent instantly available to aid in handling your relationship crises when they occur. This would be a life changer! What if Dale Carnegie could pop up on your iPad to help you solve communication hassles between you and your co-workers, family and friends? This could change your daily outlook!

Don't you wish you had the willpower of the best workout trainer, the insight of the most savvy financial investor and the organized schedule of a time management guru to help you keep your priorities straight and not get off track?

Don't you wish there were a button you could push and an entourage of bodyguards, health counselors and life coaches would remain at your disposal to help you navigate through life?

Too good to be true? The answer may surprise you. You have all these abilities at your disposal without pushing a button. These answers to life's pressing issues are found in one source—wisdom. Wisdom goes beyond intellect, common sense and the best counselor available. In fact, wisdom is so broad sweeping, it cannot be restricted merely to the scenarios I listed above. It is beyond human understanding, beyond our radarscope of logic. This is because wisdom's source is out of this world.

Most people, however (even the most mature among us), do not know how to tap in to this valuable commodity, let alone maintain it. I hope these pages will shed some light on how to accomplish those things. True wisdom helps you maximize every opportunity presented to you during your lifetime. And who would not want to live a life in the smart lane?

Supernatural Wisdom to Choose

What about my life-changing decision about whom to marry? How could I access the godly, life-changing wisdom beyond human understanding that I knew was available to me? Each woman I considered seemed compatible and companionable. I could imagine life with almost any one of them.

My story's outcome may seem unusual. For most people, it would be. But having access to the wisdom God gave me is not meant to be unusual at all, and the quest for a life partner became a turning point for me in this area. I found more than a wife; I found wisdom.

I contemplated relationships with these wonderful women from every angle. A few times I fasted, going without any food for a few days in the hopes that I would know what to do and feel certain of wisdom's answer. Yet my heart had no peace.

Back to my knees I went. Then, on December 5, 1990, after praying for several hours, I received a strong impression about the person I was to marry. No earthquake or big booming voice from heaven came, but I had a clear impression as to God's choice for me. Everything in my mind and spirit seemed to line up with the thought. It had taken four and a half years, but I finally felt sure inside. I had my answer!

I felt a sense of relief and fear simultaneously. What if I were wrong? What if I did not like her after we began a relationship? What if she refused to marry me? To complicate matters on a whole other level, I knew very little about this young woman. I knew her first name—and it was not Sally, Lydia, Marian or Cindy! This young lady, Kemi, came from Africa and took Christianity very seriously—yet that is all I knew about her.

I have to admit that I was attracted to Kemi on many levels. Her commitment to God was obvious. She was sweet, pretty and stylish. From afar, she seemed as if she had a sense of humor, and other people really liked her. These qualities were in her favor, but they were not enough; she needed to pass wisdom's scrutiny. I needed to know beyond any doubt that Kemi was the one. As I prayed about it, wisdom led me to seek a "noncoincidental" confirmation. I prayed, "God, if You are speaking Kemi to my heart, please confirm this by someone else so I can be sure." The answer was not far off.

Later that day, I called my sister Karen, who lived in another city. Halfway into our conversation about incidental family anecdotes, she said, "Oh! I had a dream about you last night. I dreamt I saw you on a large cruise ship with someone from Africa. The words *Mr. and Mrs. Africa* were written on it." Then she asked me, "Are you getting married or going to Africa? Or marrying someone from Africa?"

What were the odds of my sister experiencing such a dream on the same day I was considering marrying a girl from Africa? Amazed at God's faithfulness, I knew Karen's words bore the confirmation I needed. This was especially true since neither Karen nor anyone else had any knowledge of my thoughts—I had not told a soul.

Now everything lined up nicely. I had an absolute inner certainty—Kemi was The One. My sister's dream cemented my resolve. But it is one thing to know what God wants and another to follow through. I remember feeling surreal and thinking, *I can't believe this is happening.* I was past scared—I was shaking scared!

After a few days, I got my inner feelings and fears under control. I knew I had to pursue a course of action to see if what I felt could be right. I decided to let Kemi know what I thought during our Friday night prayer meeting. I sat away from everyone for most of the prayer time, trying to gain enough nerve to ask her. I played several scenarios over in my mind. At times I would waver and try to talk myself out of approaching her. Finally, I waxed bold, stood up and walked straight to her. I found her kneeling over a chair, praying. I tapped her on the shoulder and asked her to follow me to a quieter place.

I had to rally every nerve in my body so that I could declare, "It looks as though God is leading me to ask you to be my life partner, but I could be wrong. Please pray about it and let me know what you think."

Externally I appeared bold; internally I could not believe I was saying these words. What took all of two minutes seemed like an eternity to me. After blurting the words out, there was a moment of deep silence. Embarrassed, I almost recanted, then I heard Kemi's voice. She simply said, "Yes, sir," and quickly walked away.

"Yes, sir"—what kind of an answer was that? Mixed emotions swept over me. On the one hand, I actually felt great relief—at least my assignment was over. I also felt proud of myself for not chickening out. Even if Kemi came back and told me no, at least I had been bold enough to ask. The gnawing feeling now had been satisfied. On the other hand, I felt dismay at the prospect of what she might say. What if she did say no in the face of what I had heard from God? What then?

Kemi returned a few minutes later, interrupting my thoughts. Looking up, I was shocked to see the confidence on her face. She said, "To be honest, sir, I've known about this for some time now."

Suddenly I felt awkward. I swallowed hard and asked, "Oh, really? Do you even know my last name?"

She smiled and admitted, "No."

At this point I felt compelled to say, "Well, you'd better learn it because it will soon be your last name."

Kemi paused for a moment, smiled and left.

Sitting in the same chair for the rest of the evening, I kept thinking, *What have I just done?* But in spite of the strangeness of the events that had taken place, I felt peace. It seemed right because it was right—though not in the way your mind can manipulate you into believing something because you want it so badly. This was a peace that came from obeying God.

Kemi and I were married ten weeks later—21 years ago at the time of this writing. I am convinced that wisdom guided me in the important decision of whom to marry, and I am grateful. Wisdom's voice went beyond the thoughts of a conscience or a good dose of common sense. In fact, in this case wisdom went out of its way to prescribe an unusual course of action. I received revelation, my sister gave confirmation through a dream, I let the Word of God guide me through the story of finding Isaac's bride, and wisdom was confirmed by Kemi's affirmative answer.

Learning to gather wisdom from these sources was not instantaneous for me by any means. I had spent years finding out how wisdom worked and practicing its application. During this time I began to learn how wisdom could be measured out even to a young adult like me. I kept placing myself in the receiving position of hearing God's direction, finding how that direction should work in my life and walking in obedience to see wisdom's fruit.

The reason I believe I did not make a wrong choice is that early in my walk with God, I had decided to follow wisdom's whisper—a determination I have thanked God for continually. Wisdom did not just help me find the answer; it taught me the right questions to ask. Wisdom alerted me when something did not seem right and set me at peace when everything came into alignment.

The way God led me in this decision, not to mention how I responded, may seem unbelievable. But I believe most of us can experience more of such specific and practical methods of receiving God's wisdom—if only we understand how. At the very least, I think you can relate to my seeking the Lord for guidance and to the peace I felt at responding to the guidance I received.

Wisdom to Change Your World

Imagine what a difference just a small portion of godly wisdom could make in your life. Think about how it might affect your career or impact your choice of a mate. Imagine raising your kids using a good dose of godly wisdom. Godly wisdom improves your life regardless of your profession, your family situation and your personal circumstances. Once you have it, problems become easier to solve—a result everyone can enjoy.

Most of us appreciate wisdom's value to a certain degree, but we tend to underestimate its true worth. I would like to show you how important wisdom is. In fact, I hope that by the time you read the last page of this book, you will experience an exponential increase in how you plug in to wisdom and operate in its wake. We will also explore wisdom's benefits. God wants to bless you through His gift of wisdom. Through reading these pages, I hope your capacity to receive those blessings will increase. As you understand wisdom's inestimable importance to your life, I hope you will put considerable time and energy into seeking it.

Perhaps you, too, have experienced times when you knew that a decision you had to make would impact the rest of your life. You may even be challenged with such a decision as you read this. You cannot ignore your choices; they stand before you and demand a response. But beyond making individual decisions, you have a God-given destiny. God has a purpose for you, a path for you alone to walk on this planet. You must make many determinations along the way, and some of those will either further or hinder God's purpose for you. His wisdom can keep you on track.

You and I must depend on and trust God's wisdom. It really is not that difficult. How can we find it? Wisdom is not elusive. It may appear hidden, but it waits eagerly to be discovered. Wisdom has much to say. It stands ready to guide us in each and every decision. Following godly wisdom will allow us to shun regret.

In the chapters that follow, I will open up my life to show you how wisdom has worked for me. At times I listened to the insight I received; at times I did not and ended up paying the consequences. Through my experiences and through teaching from Scripture, I will help you learn to tap in to wisdom's inexhaustible resources so you can receive guidance and find answers. I believe you will be able to put every lesson I learned to use in your own life. You just need a few principles, some practice time and the ability to know wisdom when you see it.

I also will share how wisdom gives us insight. We will look at the fruit of wisdom in terms of intelligence, communication and making the best choices. We will examine how wisdom can create solid relationships, how we need wisdom to fulfill our priorities and how wisdom helps us live safely in a treacherous world.

Understanding the importance of wisdom is just the first step in this adventure of discovering the secrets of biblical wisdom. I am excited about taking this journey with you. In the end, I believe we all will be wiser as a result.

The next part of our adventure together will involve understanding what wisdom will produce in us once we possess it. But before we move into the next chapter, I would like to make some decrees with you concerning wisdom. In fact, woven into the text of my chapters are both decrees and prayers. My desire is that this book will impact your head and your heart. The pauses we take to reflect, pray and make decrees are designed to interrupt your train of thought so your knowledge is not limited to your head, but is also entertained in your heart.

The decrees we will make are statements or declarations that press our faith forward and crush self-doubt and fear. They help thoughts become more deeply planted in our hearts. A farmer does not leave seeds in the packets and hope they will grow. Instead, he places the seeds in the ground so they have the potential to grow. In the same way, we sow seeds—our words—by speaking them out to connect our faith with God's promises. This evokes authority both on earth and in heaven.

I include the prayers so that we take a moment to pause, humble our hearts before God and receive impartation of the principles we just covered. The act of prayer creates a window for the Holy Spirit to move on our hearts. This will cause God to work in our lives long after we finish going through this book.

I have also included questions for meditation at the end of each chapter, along with some practical tips. The questions are useful for individual study or for small group discussion. They will help you journal your adventure as you seek wisdom on a daily basis. I suggest that you devote a small notebook to recording your thoughts on this journey as God unleashes the power of more and more heavenly insight in your life.

The practical tips I include will provide some extra steps you can follow in order to actively put the principles within each chapter to use in your daily life. Some tips are suggestions to use the material directly as leverage toward exercising wisdom. Other tips will make the principles more concrete as I engage you in more specific aspects of those principles.

Let's make this first declaration together about pursuing wisdom and allowing it to transform us.

Decree of Transformation

I decree that I will strongly pursue wisdom all my days. I decree that wisdom has the power to transform me. I will let wisdom transfigure my life so that my spirit shines like the sun and becomes white as light. I decree that wisdom will consume me like fire to burn out the dross that keeps me leaning on my own understanding. May my steps be ordered so that I make divine connections and change the world through the knowledge of God. Let it be so, Father. As I have decreed, I believe You will perform these things according to Your Word. In Jesus' name, Amen.

QUESTIONS FOR MEDITATION

1. List at least three things you value in your life. How did treasuring these things affect your pursuit of them? Was it easier to practice, study or do whatever was required to excel in these areas you valued? Why? How?

33

2. Has there ever been anything in your life that you did not value at first, but began to value later? What caused you to place greater value on it? How can you apply that change in value to your pursuit of wisdom?

3. Has there ever been a time when a wise thought came to you "out of the blue" and helped you solve a perplexing problem? Jot down some things you learned from that experience.

4. Have you ever experienced a time when wisdom acted as a sentry in your life? When has wisdom emerged and helped protect you from impending danger?

5. List three areas of your life in which you could use more wisdom right now.

PRACTICAL TIPS

1. Whenever you are faced with perplexing problems, schedule dedicated think/meditation time. This could be anywhere from ten minutes to an hour. Remove yourself from noisy, distracting settings and just ponder. Perhaps take a walk in a park or along the water. Get away somewhere to relax and focus, to think and pray.

2. From your answer to meditation question 2, think about what causes you to value certain things. Consider the methods you use to pursue them. Write out how you can apply the same strategy to valuing and pursuing wisdom.

3. Read and memorize wisdom quotes and literature. Start with a chapter a day from the book of Proverbs. There

are 31 chapters, so you can read through the book in a month. After Proverbs, read through Ecclesiastes and Song of Songs. Then search for other wisdom literature. You will find that as you saturate your mind with such wisdom, it will emerge as needed and assist you.

4. Stress and anxiety often drown out wisdom's whisper. Maintain a calm, peaceful inner life as much as possible by trusting God. When you begin to feel tension or a negative emotion, take a moment to declare your trust in God to your spirit.

2

Wisdom's Playbook

> We can be knowledgeable with other men's
> knowledge, but we cannot be wise with other
> men's wisdom.
>
> —Montaigne

A s a young boy something always fascinated me about church, God and religion. I lived in New York City with my mom and dad, neither of whom went to church. During the summers I would sometimes visit my grandmother in Tuskegee, Alabama, who did little else but go to church. I am not exaggerating—she went to church, the grocery store and home. Not only did she go to her church; she also went to everyone else's church where there was a special program or revival. During the summers, I was with her at all of these church services. Somehow I loved it. I was fixated most of the time on the preaching. I loved to hear stories expounded from the Scriptures. Everything seemed to stick to me—I was being shaped, although I did not know it.

During those days, I heard what would become my lifetime favorite Scripture. I heard it first read by a pastor in one of those small rural churches we would visit. It was the 23rd Psalm. One reason I loved it so much was because it was authored by David, the little boy who killed the big giant. Additionally, the preacher quoted it in a magical, poetic way, like many of the old country preachers in Tuskegee. They used a combination of a slow, rhyming speech with a booming, accented baritone voice. Of course, this was intermixed with "Amen!" and "Hallelujah!" shouted from the congregation. The whole experience was as exhilarating as a high-paced action movie, but the spiritual component made me feel the impact deeply. When the service concluded, I could not wait to get home and read the psalm for myself in our huge coffee-table Bible Grandma kept in the living room. I ran in and quickly turned her King James Version of the Bible to Psalm 23 and read,

> The LORD is my shepherd; I shall not want.
> He maketh me to lie down in green pastures: he leadeth me beside the still waters.
> He restoreth my soul: he leadeth me in the paths of righteousness for his name's sake.
> Yea, though I walk through the valley of the shadow of death, I will fear no evil: for thou art with me; thy rod and thy staff they comfort me.
> Thou preparest a table before me in the presence of mine enemies: thou anointest my head with oil; my cup runneth over.
> Surely goodness and mercy shall follow me all the days of my life: and I will dwell in the house of the LORD for ever.

Once I read it, I became thoroughly confused. It made no sense to me. I was puzzled beyond measure as to how the

Lord could be such a good Shepherd who did all of those good things like making us lie down in green pastures and leading us beside still waters, and yet David did not want Him. It said clearly on the page, "The LORD is my shepherd; I shall not want." I was seriously baffled, but instead of asking someone, I tried to figure it out on my own. I kept reading the psalm over and over, looking for some clue as to why David would reject such a great Shepherd. After a few days of searching, I gave up and asked Grandma. She explained that the true meaning of the word *want* in this verse is "no lack." I finally understood that David was actually saying that he would have no lack because his Shepherd would supply everything he needed.

This lesson taught me the importance of understanding proper definitions. Wisdom's definition is one we ought to understand.

The Playbook's First Page

As we define wisdom, it is important to understand that there are two basic spiritual sources of wisdom. These are:

1. God's wisdom, which is heavenly wisdom from above (see 1 Corinthians 2:6–7; James 1:17).
2. Counterfeit wisdom, which is demonic wisdom from beneath (James 3:15).

Both of these spiritual sources of wisdom seek expression through humanity. They are both available to tap in to whenever wisdom is needed.

I spend the majority of this book's pages constructing the place, the Person and the power of true godly wisdom. But I also will help you understand the source of false wisdom so you can avoid it. We must learn to recognize demonic wisdom so we can see the snake coming before it arrives. We will talk about this in more detail in chapter 8, "Wisdom Comes Clean." But until then, stick this knowledge in the back of your mind: You will need to learn how to recognize false wisdom when it crosses your path.

One sure sign of true wisdom is that it does not just live for the moment. True wisdom considers the end as well. It contemplates how others are affected by what is being done. True wisdom is married to good behavior and deeds. It has an internal code of conduct that is inseparable from them.

The character of wisdom, however, does not completely explain its meaning. Zeroing in on wisdom is like trying to define the scientific principles of gravity. We know gravity exists. We sense its presence in all we do. We understand the physical effects of its law on us. Yet we cannot see, touch or taste gravity. In the same way, we experience wisdom in different dimensions as we navigate life's path, yet we cannot confine it to a book, a three-by-five index card or a written prayer.

Wisdom may seem somewhat elusive, yet we must learn to recognize its presence when it impacts us. There are many counterfeits to wisdom, but we will know true wisdom by its fruit. In this book, I will put wisdom under a microscope to examine its DNA so we can easily recognize it. However, we need to look first at its more obvious characteristics. This will build a foundation for the chapters that follow.

The Playbook's Rules on Wisdom

As we look at the truth about wisdom, we need to flesh out how it operates, how it manifests and the by-products or fruits that are borne out of it. Wisdom is not automated. You must learn how to access and operate in it. In this chapter I will share a few of the rules in wisdom's playbook. For example, you might ask, "Does wisdom just mean being 'Smarter Than a 5th Grader'? Is wisdom choosing the best course of action?" We can shed some light on these questions by looking at the Greek word for wisdom in *Strong's Exhaustive Concordance of the Bible*. It is *sophia* [sof-ee-ah], which means "wisdom, broad and full of intelligence; used of the knowledge of very diverse matters. The wisdom which belongs to men."[1]

What is unique about this word is the next part of the definition: "The varied knowledge of things human and divine, acquired by acuteness and experience, and summed up in maxims and proverbs." This tells us that wisdom is both human and divine knowledge, not just the learning gained at a certain grade level. *Strong's* definition goes on: "The science and learning. The act of interpreting dreams and always giving the sagest advice. The intelligence evinced in discovering the meaning of some mysterious number or vision. Skill in the management of affairs." This part of the definition shows how all-encompassing wisdom is. It is not limited to one discipline of learning. It is global in nature.

The next part of the definition connects wisdom to faith: "Devout and proper prudence in intercourse with men, skill and discretion in imparting Christian truth. The knowledge and practice of the requisites for godly and upright living."

Wisdom creates an aptitude for holiness and moral character. It works almost like acquiring a taste for a favorite food or a craving for a specific activity or person. However, many people feed unhealthy cravings in unhealthy ways. For example, some crave money to the point of engaging in immoral, unholy behavior. This type of behavior distinguishes wisdom that comes from a source other than God.

The final part of *Strong's* definition for *sophia* connects wisdom with authority and earthly leadership: "Supreme intelligence, such as belongs to God. The wisdom of God as evinced in forming and executing counsels in the formation and government of the world and the scriptures." Here we see heaven touching earth in the governance of mankind.

From these definitions and our practical experience, we see that wisdom cannot just be compared to the knowledge of a 5th grader or a Ph.D. graduate. It is more than knowledge, while not absent of knowledge. Wisdom works better if you have ample knowledge, but knowledge is not a prerequisite. Most of us have heard of, and perhaps met, people with amazing amounts of knowledge but not enough practical sense to function normally. In the chapters that follow, look for the intelligence factor in the wisdom examples from Scripture and in the true-life stories. Sometimes you will find a heavy dose of intelligence to go along with wisdom. Other times, however, you will observe that a scant helping of brainpower was involved.

Wisdom and Common Sense

Clearly, wisdom is more than knowledge or intelligence. At this point, I want to make another distinction—this time between wisdom and common sense. Is wisdom simply applying sound reasoning to a situation? Let's explore this a bit deeper.

One Hebrew word the Bible translates as wisdom is *sekel* [I-kel], which *Strong's Exhaustive Concordance* describes as: "prudence, insight, understanding, good sense, cunning, craft (bad sense)."[2] Just as in the case of knowledge or intelligence, wisdom certainly enhances common sense—but it is not common sense alone. Having common sense may be the way most would describe a person who just acted wisely, but when it comes to wisdom, there is more taking place under the surface. For example, at times wisdom may provide information neither learned nor deduced by practical reasoning. Wisdom often has a revelatory component. Information revealed by wisdom is spot-on. This is not just common sense—it is wisdom; head-turning wisdom at that. Some refer to this as the "supernatural gift of wisdom." Such wisdom is not acquired through experience or study—it is given by revelation and allows you to see life and situations from God's perspective. At times it can even reveal future things impossible to know in the present, giving you the advantage of "seeing over the hill," so to speak.

Wisdom is also results oriented. Dr. David Oyedepo, in his book *The Wisdom That Works*, says,

> Wisdom is the best way to get things done. It is the most effective way to accomplishing a task; the least stressful way to getting results; the most cost effective way to securing solutions to challenging problems. Wisdom is about works not words. Words they say are cheap. But work is what defines the worth of wisdom.[3]

Wisdom is a deep understanding of and realization about people, things, events and situations that result in the ability to choose or act in a manner that consistently produces optimal results with minimum time and energy. Read that sentence again. Now pause and take it in. This wisdom certainly is something every person would desire. Let's go before God and seek Him for such wisdom. As I mentioned in chapter 1, praying together throughout this book will create a window for the Holy Spirit to move on our hearts both now and long after we are finished with these pages.

Prayer for Supernatural Wisdom

Heavenly Father, I ask You in the name of Jesus to grant me a good supply of supernatural wisdom. Grant me greater revelation, that I might see what I need to see. Let me understand events and relationships so that I might apply common sense to the situations I face. Help me use wisdom to serve those around me. I ask that You be generous and liberal in supplying wisdom to me. Let it be noticeable to those who know me. In Jesus' name, Amen.

Wisdom Makes Priorities

Time management is an essential quality of success. The limit of hours we have each day creates decision trees of cause and effect. Fulfilling obligations in priority order has become extremely important. Wisdom benefits you by helping you choose the best course of action in every circumstance.

One note of caution: The best course of action might not be what is pleasant or desirable in satisfying yourself. Jesus went to the cross—an event that caused Him great pain and agony—yet it was the wisdom of God that chose such a strategy for salvation (see 1 Corinthians 1:21–24). Wisdom's path may not always lead you to the most pleasant course of action. It will often require you to sacrifice for others. In other words, wisdom is not meant only to serve you for your benefit; it also will deliver the best outcome for others in any situation.

Wisdom provides you with the ability to apply optimally (effectively and efficiently) perceptions and knowledge so as to produce the desired results. Wisdom is insight into the true nature of things, which enables you to act in a way that produces the highest productivity and profit.

Wisdom's Accessibility

I have had a few people ask me if wisdom is solely a spiritual gift. Are wise people born that way? Can a foolish person become wise? One great thing about wisdom is that it is accessible to all. The Scriptures give a clear invitation to anyone who lacks wisdom: "If any of you lacks wisdom, he should ask God, who gives generously to all without finding fault, and it will be given to him" (James 1:5).

We recognize that some are born with special gifts others do not have. Some are musical geniuses like Beethoven and Mozart. Others find it hard to compete with such musical genius even though they love music. Still others are more left-brain dominant and do well with math and scientific thought, whereas right-brain dominant individuals excel in the arts and in activities requiring spatial thought. Though we are all born with special graces, wisdom is available to all of us in a variety of areas. According to the verse above and other Scriptures, we need but ask and it will be given generously.

Specificity of Wisdom

One great thing about wisdom is its application to overarching life rules or principles, as well as to individual situations. This is because of the three-fold nature of wisdom. Merriam-Webster defines *wisdom* as knowledge, insight and judgment.[4] The knowledge component of wisdom is accumulated learning. Insight is the ability to discern inner or hidden issues. Judgment refers to good sense.

These three components, working in unpredictable combinations, summarize wisdom. At times, wisdom may manifest itself as an opportunity to use what you have previously learned. Most of us have probably experienced a time when something we learned, read or thought about long ago suddenly, almost miraculously, comes to mind right when we need it. At other times, wisdom surfaces as information you previously did not know, but instantly discern. Often wisdom emerges almost as an epiphany. It is as if a lightbulb comes on and you see what should have been apparent before. Now it is clear since wisdom has kicked in.

Revelation and Wisdom

Two Hebrew words for *wisdom* describe it in very natural terms. As you read each word's definition, look at the character needed to put wisdom to use and the importance of wisdom's timing. One word is *tuwshiyah* [too·shee·yaw], which means "sound knowledge, success, sound or efficient wisdom, abiding success."[5] The other is *leb* [labe], which means "inner man, mind, will, heart, understanding. Heart (of man). Soul (of man). Mind, knowledge, thinking, reflection, memory. Inclination, resolution, determination (of will). Conscience. Heart (of moral character). Seat of appetites. Seat of emotions and passions. Seat of courage."[6]

The great thing about wisdom is that it combines the knowledge of God with the knowledge of men to produce revelation and insight beyond the scope of any guru or sage. Who is the wisest person who every lived, besides Jesus? The wisest human being in history received his wisdom by asking for it. First Kings 3 records a dialogue between God and King Solomon in a dream. God asked Solomon a question I have longed to be asked: "Ask for whatever *you want* me to give you" (verse 5, emphasis added). Amazing! This is almost like the genie coming out of the bottle and asking for your wish, only there was no genie—this was God Almighty, Himself!

Solomon responded, "Give your servant a discerning heart to govern your people and to distinguish between right and wrong. For who is able to govern this great people of yours?" (verse 9).

God asked Solomon to name whatever he wanted, but make no mistake—God asked this question because of what He already knew about Solomon. This would be a very dangerous question otherwise. God knew Solomon already had enough wisdom to choose a wise question. Solomon's small amount of wisdom caused him to ask for more wisdom.

God was pleased with Solomon's request and answered the prayer immediately. King Solomon literally woke up the next day as the wisest man of his time. Through this wisdom, Solomon led Israel to the greatest, most prosperous period in the country's history. Through wisdom, he had the capacity to make choices that caused everything he touched to blossom.

Wisdom Put to the Test

King Solomon was about eighteen years old when he became Israel's king. One of the first challenges he faced was a dilemma between two women arguing over a baby. One woman's baby had died, and both women claimed the living baby who remained as their own. King Solomon's wisdom shone a brilliant light on the situation. In the court proceeding, both ladies presented their case. Since DNA testing was nonexistent and no witnesses could affirm whom the living baby belonged to, King Solomon had to rely on wisdom:

> The king said, "This one says, 'My son is alive and your son is dead,' while that one says, 'No! Your son is dead and mine is alive.'"
>
> Then the king said, "Bring me a sword." So they brought a sword for the king. He then gave an order: "Cut the living child in two and give half to one and half to the other."
>
> 1 Kings 3:23–25

I cringe just thinking about the gruesome act that might have followed. Yet Solomon's wisdom taught him that a mother's love is so strong that she would not want her child to die regardless of the circumstances. Here is how the story played out:

The woman whose son was alive was filled with compassion for her son and said to the king, "Please, my lord, give her the living baby! Don't kill him!"

But the other said, "Neither I nor you shall have him. Cut him in two!"

Then the king gave his ruling: "Give the living baby to the first woman. Do not kill him; she is his mother."

1 Kings 3:26–27

The comments both women made resulted from King Solomon's wise course of action and revealed who was the true mother. A true mother would never harm her child, loving him even to the point of giving him up to another. As a result of Solomon's decision, "When all Israel heard the verdict the king had given, they held the king in awe, because they saw that he had wisdom from God to administer justice" (1 Kings 3:28).

Solomon exhibited a healthy dose of *chokmah*, another Hebrew word for *wisdom*. According to *Strong's*, *chokmah* [khokmaw] is "skill (in war), wisdom (in administration). Shrewdness, prudence (in religious affairs). Wisdom in (ethical and religious situations)."[7] This wisdom came in handy for Solomon!

Wisdom's Playbook Is Universal

Kings are not the only ones who need this level of wisdom. We need it, too. Every day of our lives, situations confront us in which we need to solve problems. These dilemmas may not play out as graphically as the story in 1 Kings 3, but our challenges are still producing stress and its side effects in our lives.

Parents need this level of wisdom to properly raise their children. Bosses need this wisdom to prudently lead their employees. Schoolteachers need this wisdom to appropriately instruct students and to administer discipline. Businesspeople need this wisdom to see what is behind proposed contracts and delayed invoices. The list goes on and on. We need wisdom because we have problems that are perplexing. Wisdom turns perplexing problems into perfect solutions.

Increased productivity is a measure of true wisdom. As I stated previously, wisdom can be understood, but it is difficult to narrow down to a scientific definition. We can know when wisdom is in operation because wisdom's product determines its presence. When good fruit is produced, wisdom is most likely behind the curtain.

I hope you are inspired to push distractions and unproductive activities out of your way and race to embrace wisdom's bounty. In the next chapter, we will look at how wisdom speaks to us. I want to share some of the insight I have received through wisdom's voice. Before I do that, though, let's make the following decree as an act of faith. Then take a few minutes to answer the questions for meditation as a way to assess how well you understand the word *wisdom*.

Decree for Wisdom

Lord, I decree that wisdom will be drawn to me like a magnet to metal. Make us inseparable. By faith, I declare that when I need wisdom, it will be provided. I open my mind and heart to Your tender touch. Thank You, Lord, for providing wisdom when I need it. In Jesus' name, Amen.

QUESTIONS FOR MEDITATION

1. Look through this chapter for the one Greek word and four Hebrew words that are translated as *wisdom* in Scripture. Highlight the definitions that apply to you today. Take a moment in prayer to examine how God

might want you to remember these words and amplify them in your daily life.

2. Have you ever asked any questions about wisdom similar to the questions in this chapter? If so, which ones stand out to you the most? Did the brief answers help you understand the principles behind wisdom? (Remember these principles will be covered in depth in the chapters that follow.)

3. If God asked you the same question that He asked Solomon, what would you answer? Would your answer be dotted with Kingdom purpose or with something more self-serving?

4. Solomon's acute sense of right and wrong came into play as he made his decision in the court case between the two mothers claiming the same baby. How do you think Solomon received his peculiar course of action? Through revelation, intelligence, insight, common sense . . . or something else?

PRACTICAL TIPS

1. Most of us have faced times when people have tried to pull something over on us or when we have not chosen wisely. We must check, double-check and triple-check before we make weighty decisions that have far-reaching effects. The Holy Spirit is never in a hurry unless there is danger involved.

2. Pulling wisdom into our lives means we must be aware of God's ability to be present in every moment of our

day. Give yourself a reminder of this every hour at an odd time such as 22 minutes after the hour. This will make you remember and look forward to the next time you can stop what you are doing for just 60 seconds and seek God.

3. Create a short list of the wisest people you know. What makes you think they are wise? What fruits or benefits of wisdom do you observe in their lives? Take time to contact these people over the next week or so and ask how they received their wisdom. Then ask God what truths you should learn from their answers.

4. The dictionary definition of *wisdom* is worth remembering: Wisdom is knowledge, insight and judgment. Write this on a card and memorize it.

3

‖‖‖‖‖‖‖‖‖‖‖‖‖‖‖‖‖‖‖‖‖‖‖‖‖‖‖‖‖‖‖‖‖‖

Wisdom

The Insight Whisperer

A moment's insight is sometimes worth a life's experience.

—Oliver Wendell Holmes Jr.

I became born-again as a senior in college. I was ready to receive my commission in the United States Air Force as a second lieutenant, but a few months before the commissioning, something strange began to happen—I came under heavy guilt. I suddenly knew God was real and that my life was not right in His sight. I was not living what many would say was a "really bad" life. I did not take or sell drugs, but I did have my vices. I was profane in my language—extremely profane! I did not practice sexual abstinence; waiting until marriage was not for me. I would lie a bit more than occasionally. Oh, and did I mention that I cheated on tests every now and then? On second thought, maybe I was a really bad guy.

Whatever you may think of my life back then, the Holy Spirit let me know what He thought. He descended on me with strong conviction. I began to weep almost every night and ask God to forgive me for my sins. After about three weeks of this pattern, I finally felt relieved of my burden. I asked Jesus to come into my life, saying, "Jesus, You are real! I give You 100 percent of my life."

This experience meant so much to me that I was willing to give up anything and everything for Him. I felt whole for the first time in my life. The world seemed perfect; I felt as if I had no needs. Nothing mattered but my newfound faith, and I wanted everyone to know about it. Thanks to special legislation enacted to reduce the size of the military forces, I was able to say no to my Air Force career. I elected instead to stay in Montgomery, Alabama, and share Jesus with anyone who would listen.

My first job after graduation was as a dorm director at my alma mater. It was an easy job. All I had to do was walk around and make sure everything was safe and in order between 10:00 P.M. and 6:00 A.M. Yet there was a problem. During the day, when I should have been sleeping, I kept busy evangelizing students. I spent the day teaching Bible studies, and I witnessed to people until it was time to go to work. I would clock in at 10:00 and spend time sharing Christ and praying with students until they went to sleep—usually around midnight. Then I was left alone in the office with a desk, two chairs and a comfortable new sofa.

For the first few weeks I would try to fight off the temptation, but eventually I gave in . . . the sofa won. Somewhere between 1:00 and 2:00 A.M., I crawled up on the sofa and slept until about 5:00. I rationalized that this was okay because I was doing God's work during the day. Surely God was pleased and would take care of any repercussions. After all, He knew I was tired from serving Him.

One day, I was shocked to find out that I was no longer employed. It confounded me. I thought, *God, is this how You repay me for serving You?* I laugh when I think about how ridiculous that sounds, but my reasoning at the time was very convoluted.

There had been times that wisdom whispered insight to me as I lay my head down: *This is not right; you should give an honest day's work for an honest day's pay.* But I ignored these quiet inner nudges, thinking my reasoning was superior. Scripture also spoke to me, giving insight that I was wrong. But I ignored verses such as, "Whatever your hand finds to do, do it with all your might" (Ecclesiastes 9:10).

I certainly was not performing the duties required of a dorm director with all my might. I admit I slept pretty hard on that sofa, but I am sure that is not what the verse was implying that I do with all my might! Another verse that surfaced in my thoughts was, "Whatever you do, work at it with all your heart, as working for the Lord, not for men" (Colossians 3:23). Working for the Lord was really not separate from working for men, and certainly I was not laboring with all my heart at my job. Next the Golden Rule showed up in my devotional time: "Do to others as you would have them do to you" (Luke 6:31). I know I would not want to pay someone who worked for me to sleep, so why did I think the university should approve of my behavior?

During this time I also gained insight into a fact that should have straightened me out. From time to time my boss would check on me at night. I never saw him, but I sensed it. He never said anything, but I knew it. Even if I ignored everything else, the likelihood that I would be caught should have caused me to change my behavior. But remember, I was tired from doing "God's work" all day, which surpassed everything else—or so I thought. After I lost my job, my boss verified my suspicion. He told me that he knew I had been sleeping on the job.

Each of these whisperings of wisdom spoke to me quietly. I ignored them all. I received insight into my behavior and disregarded it, and as a result, I paid a price. Not only was I embarrassed by losing a job, but I was a Christian who had been fired. Worst of all, I was also broke. What testimony did I have with those in higher management now? If only I had listened to the insight wisdom had given me.

Wisdom Sees around the Corner

Not only does wisdom whisper to your spiritual ears, wisdom can also give "sight" to your spiritual eyes. Wisdom causes you to see what is unapparent to others. You have probably heard the saying, "In the land of the blind, the one-eyed man is king." If wisdom can help you see just a little bit better than the mainstream, it will position you to soar. Wisdom releases insight into the true nature of things. The description of what God did for Solomon when he asked for wisdom helps us understand insight:

> God gave Solomon wisdom and very great insight, and a *breadth of understanding* as measureless as the sand on the seashore. Solomon's wisdom was greater than the wisdom of all the men of the East, and greater than all the wisdom of Egypt. . . . He spoke three thousand proverbs and his songs numbered a thousand and five. He described plant life, from the cedar of Lebanon to the hyssop that grows out of walls. He also taught about animals and birds, reptiles and fish.
>
> 1 Kings 4:29–33, emphasis added

Solomon began to receive true insight into the nature of things previously unknown. That is the power of wisdom. Wisdom sees beyond what the average person sees. It reveals the true nature of things, allowing you to understand what natural deduction and reasoning could not reveal. It sees what is hidden and discerns the obscure. It reveals the what, when, where, how and why of any situation.

Adam experienced great insight during creation:

> Now the LORD God had formed out of the ground all the beasts of the field and all the birds of the air. He brought them to the man to see what he would name them; and whatever the man called each living creature, that was its name. So the man gave names to all the livestock, the birds of the air and all the beasts of the field.
>
> Genesis 2:19–20

When Adam named the animals, he did not just pick arbitrary names out of the *New World Creation Dictionary*. He actually examined each creature's character and chose a name that represented its character. Through wisdom and insight Adam saw into the true nature of these creatures.

I often imagine God and Adam spending time together viewing creation. I picture God showing Adam deep secrets and insights into the instinctive nature of the animals. I imagine God presenting one of His creatures to Adam, and Adam smiling and then gasping at God's handiwork. Adam asks a few clarifying questions, then God says, "Adam, My son, what do you want to call this one?" Adam contemplates the nature and purpose of this new being, and he seeks to match that nature and purpose with words and concepts. Finally, he arrives at a name.

George Washington Carver, the famous black scientist who lived in the late 1800s and early 1900s, created more than four hundred extremely useful products from peanuts and sweet potatoes. He created everything from gasoline to medicine. Was he just smarter than most? Or did he have some kind of special insight into the nature of these items?

Obviously, God granted Carver wisdom to see into the nature of things. Carver himself shared how this came to be. One day he asked God to show him the secrets of the universe. God said to his heart, "That is too big for you."

Then Carver asked God to show him the secrets of man. God again replied, "That is too big for you."

Finally, Carver said, "Then show me the secrets of the peanut."

God said, "That is something you can handle."

From that time on, Carver was given insight and foresight that caused him to make new products from the peanut and bring them into plain sight.[1]

Jesus often had insight into what was behind certain questions asked of Him during His earthly ministry. People often attempted to trap Him with questions; then they waited for the wrong answer so they could condemn Him. Jesus had so many enemies that one wrong reply out of His mouth could have been detrimental to His public ministry. On one occasion, a member of the antagonistic religious sect called the Pharisees approached Him and said, "We know you are a man of integrity and that you teach the way of God in accordance with the truth. You aren't swayed by men, because you pay no attention to who they are. Tell us then, what is your opinion? Is it right to pay taxes to Caesar or not?" (Matthew 22:16–17).

This may seem like an innocent question on the surface, but it was fully loaded. The Jews hated paying tax to the Roman Gentile power. Moreover, Caesar was revered as a god. If Jesus had said, "Pay your taxes to Caesar," He would have angered and alienated the Jews. However, if Jesus had said, "Don't pay taxes," He would have enraged the Romans. Either answer would have cost Him significantly.

This question would have mystified many who depended on earthly reasoning to answer, but Jesus, full of wisdom, had insight into the true nature of the question. He knew the what, the why and the how. He saw the evil intent of His questioners' hearts. Jesus responded,

> "You hypocrites, why are you trying to trap me? Show me the coin used for paying the tax." They brought him a denarius, and he asked them, "Whose portrait is this? And whose inscription?"
>
> "Caesar's," they replied.
>
> Then he said to them, "Give to Caesar what is Caesar's, and to God what is God's."
>
> Matthew 22:18–21

Jesus confounded His enemies. When they heard His answer, they were amazed. There was nothing they could say, so they simply "left him and went away" (verse 22). Before we move on, let's pray for the kind of amazing wisdom and insight that Adam, Solomon and most of all, Jesus displayed.

Prayer for Wisdom

Father, give me keen discernment and breadth of mind so that I can function at the capacity You gave Adam before the Fall. Allow my mind to absorb, process, categorize and apply knowledge in line with the heart of a matter or situation and with the skill set of Christ Jesus. Your Word declares that I have the mind of Christ; therefore, no problem is beyond my capability because Your Spirit illuminates my thoughts with divine revelation and enlightens the eyes of my understanding. Lord, may You be fully glorified in me as I express Your intelligence and wisdom in my life to benefit my family, place of business, school, church and community. In Jesus' name, Amen.

Wisdom Revealed

One of the greatest needs of our day is wisdom coupled with revelation. God is constantly communicating insights to His children. His communication comes to us in many ways. He uses dreams, visions, the Scriptures and the inward witness of our hearts, to name just a few. Since Christianity is a relationship as opposed to a religion, it is essential that we hear and see the present-tense working of the Lord in our lives. We must learn to "trust in the LORD with all your heart and lean not on your own understanding; in all your ways acknowledge him, and he will make your paths straight" (Proverbs 3:5–6).

We must acknowledge God in all our ways, expecting that He will direct our paths. God constantly wants to show us what path we should take. A person facing the possibility of three jobs wants to know which one is best. He or she may be able to decide by reasoning alone, but there are always some unknowns that are imperative to know. God knows how long the company will last. He knows how the stock will perform. He knows the pitfalls and problems the company will encounter. God knows the future, and we do not. Our natural inclination would probably be to choose the job with the highest income and best benefits, but that might not be best for us overall.

You may think, *How in the world could the highest income and greatest benefits not be best?* There could be a myriad of reasons. The job might be so demanding that it would deplete your time with your spouse and children—the last thing you need. A health hazard could be present, perhaps a chemical in the plant that would negatively affect your allergies and result in severe health challenges. The company could be on the road to bankruptcy a few months ahead. Perhaps in a little while a change of management would occur, and the new management would run the company down.

Do you get the picture? God knows what lies ahead—He knows the unknowns—so it is best to acknowledge Him and let Him guide you.

The Whisper of Revelation

When God makes His will known to man, it is called revelation. When we receive revelation, it must be tempered with wisdom. In my 24 years of being a minister, I have met many who understood the principle of seeking God to know His will but who made a mess of things by not balancing their revelation with wisdom. This same thing almost caused me to make a huge mistake with our church back when our membership was around 300. While in prayer one day, I began to imagine a 3,000-seat sanctuary that belonged to our church. The more I imagined it, the more it became real to me. I felt God was asking me to build the building etched in my mind.

Extremely excited, I set out to fulfill this "heavenly vision" I had witnessed. I set up a meeting with a major contractor to help the church make this project come to pass. We were going to build a 3,000-seat sanctuary! We hired an architect to design the building. We purchased land at an unbelievably great price, which further convinced me that we were on the right track.

As we moved forward, occasionally Frank Manuel, our church contractor, would ask, "Pastor, are you sure we need to build a 3,000-seat sanctuary? We only have a few hundred people."

I would reply, "Oh yes, Brother Frank, I saw it in a vision."

Frank would say, "Yes, sir," but I am sure he walked away shaking his head and thinking, *This course of action just doesn't seem wise.*

Frank eventually presented the price tag for our new building—five million dollars. I am sure he thought that number would wake me up, but it did not move me a bit because I had seen the "heavenly vision." It did not bother me that our total annual income was only a few hundred thousand dollars; I was committed to what my vision showed me.

What I failed to realize is that God often shows you the end from the beginning. When God shows you something, there may be a significant delay between the time He reveals it and the time it occurs. For example, God burdened Moses' heart to deliver the children of Israel. The burden was so strong that Moses killed an Egyptian early on to fulfill it—an impulsive and unwarranted murder. He was attempting to express the burden of his heart for Israel, but he acted in his own strength. God did use Moses to deliver Israel according to His plan—forty years later.

Another example is King David, who was anointed king when he was about seventeen years old. Yet the fulfillment of the anointing ceremony did not occur until David was forty. He was given a promise, but the realization of it was a long way off.

I was familiar with these two examples from the Bible, yet it never dawned on me that the building I was imagining could be a future plan that did not need an immediate response. One morning, however, I awoke feeling very uneasy. I was suddenly struck with a sense that we might be headed in the wrong direction.

Since Frank had been trying to speak wisdom to me throughout the process, I called to meet with him. As we talked, he began to lay out a wise strategy. He said, "Pastor, I know and believe God will give us the very building you imagined, but could that be in the future? Since our attendance and budget is relatively small, maybe we should just take the next step and build a multipurpose building we can afford. Then we can plan toward the bigger building at a later time."

Frank's words made sense to me. "That's wisdom!" I exclaimed.

At 4870 Woodley Road in Montgomery sits a 22,500-square-foot building that houses a 600-seat sanctuary. That building is the result of my meeting that day with Frank. We outgrew our Woodley Road building in a few years, and now we worship in a 2,200-seat sanctuary. Can you guess how many seats will be in the next sanctuary we have? Perhaps 3,000 or more! The vision is coming to pass, but it was not meant to be fulfilled the day it came.

I learned a great lesson from Frank. Revelation that is not measured by wisdom can result in a mess. I am convinced that had I persisted in that early path of insisting that the vision happen immediately, I could have caused the church great harm. I thank God that He caused me to listen to wisdom. Take a moment to pray so that you might listen as wisdom speaks into your life.

Prayer to Hear Wisdom's Voice

Father, I come to You in the name of Jesus, asking that You help me yield to wisdom's suggestions. Adjust my inner radar to know when I am presented with a wise option or strategy. Help me match biblical truth with sound counsel and ideas that I receive. Help me avoid unnecessary pain by heeding wisdom's suggestions. In Jesus' name, Amen.

Paul's Whisper of Wisdom

Wisdom and revelation appear together in Paul's prayer for the church at Ephesus: "I keep asking that the God of our Lord Jesus Christ, the glorious Father, may give you the Spirit of wisdom and revelation, so that you may know him better" (Ephesians 1:17).

Paul's prayer can be interpreted as someone asking that wisdom and revelation will produce more knowledge in us about Christ. It can also be interpreted as asking God for wisdom and revelation into the knowledge He has about particular situations. Either way you interpret it, clearly wisdom and revelation are related. They are from the same Source.

Revelation is when God makes known information or understanding previously unknown. I do not believe it is possible to have true wisdom from above without a revelatory component attached. It gives me hope to see that Solomon had more than knowledge—he had wisdom founded on revelation. If the wisdom he displayed were simply knowledge that he had or some special skill for gaining information, I might lack the faith to pursue wisdom. However, if it was revelation he received or a hearing ear, then I can believe it is possible for me to receive it as well—and so can you. Such things are only given as a gift and not by merit. Therefore, you and I qualify!

Wisdom working through the Spirit of revelation has occurred a few times in my life. One such example benefited me financially. In 1992, I was working as a suit salesman in a discount department store. That year, the company's stock was about to go public. Before the public offering, they gave the employees the opportunity to invest in an IPO (initial public offering) and buy stock at a discounted rate. I had never purchased stock before, so I prayed. As I prayed, a strong impression entered my mind: "Buy the stock at $11 per share, and it will double. Then sell it."

I decided to take a risk and yield to the impression. I scrounged up enough money to buy 150 shares. Within two years, the stock doubled. Once again, that same impression came: "Sell the stock." I sold the stock for exactly $22 per share. I was a happy suit salesman! In this instance, wisdom was coupled with revelation. I received revelation about what was going to happen and wisdom about how to capitalize on it. The two working together produced highly favorable results.

Solomon Heard the Whisper

In chapter 2, I shared the story of King Solomon asking God for wisdom. He prayed, "So give your servant a *discerning heart* to govern your people and to distinguish between right and wrong. For who is able to govern this great people of yours?" (1 Kings 3:9, emphasis added).

The Hebrew word used for *heart* in the above verse is *shama*.[2] It means a hearing ear. When Solomon asked for a discerning heart, he was asking for the ability to hear what was on *God's* heart. Solomon was asking for an unbroken connection between God and himself that allowed him to hear what he needed to hear, when he needed it. He was basically asking for continuous access to an instantaneous flow of revelation. This prayer leads me to conclude that the dispensing of Solomon's wisdom was different than some might think. God did not simply enlarge Solomon's brain or store more information in it. Perhaps that happened to some degree, but something more was happening. It was not just storage of information, but rather an open pathway of continual revelation.

Solomon demonstrated his hearing ear when the Queen of Sheba came "to test him with hard questions" (1 Kings 10:1).

I am sure she asked Solomon questions about nature and life in general. Perhaps she presented architectural riddles as well as scientific myths. Maybe she simply communed with him about the issues of romance and human relationships. We do not know the exact nature of her questions. What we do know is that "she came to Solomon and talked with him about all that she had on her mind. Solomon answered all her questions; nothing was too hard for the king to explain to her" (1 Kings 10:2–3).

Wow! Nothing was too hard for Solomon to answer. Nothing was concealed from him. Notice the verses do not say that there was nothing he did not already know, nor do they imply that there was nothing he had not already studied. Whether he was familiar with the topics she brought up or not, he was able to give her an answer. This was insight at its best.

When I was a teenager, I experienced wisdom based on insight. At the time, I am not sure I really could have identified insight as my partner. I probably thought it was luck. But it was wisdom that was most beneficial.

Burger King was the first fast-food restaurant built in Tuskegee. My friends and I hung out there several times a week—but at the age of seventeen I wanted to become an employee. I walked in, asked for the manager on duty and told her I was seeking employment. She hired me on the spot. It was my first major job. I had maintained a few other odd jobs sweeping a store and throwing papers, but this was a "real job"—or so my teenage mind reasoned.

I set out to make a good impression. I worked diligently, going above and beyond anything they asked me to do. Butch, the store owner/manager, was a hard, mean man. He would often chew out employees in front of the whole team. He was difficult to please. This made my job even more challenging—but I was determined to succeed. I started out doing janitorial work, but quickly moved up to working in the kitchen. In a short time I was promoted to working the cash register and taking orders.

One day while I was working the register, Butch asked me to bring a few large bills to the office so he could give me change. It was early morning, and the largest bills I had were a few twenties. I took him three $20 bills and watched him as he carefully counted the change. He even counted it twice. As I watched, I realized he had given me an extra $5 bill. I walked back to my register with two distinct but diverse thoughts entering my mind. The first was, *He gave you five dollars too much and didn't realize it; just take it.* I had never taken money from a cash register before, so this was a strange thought to me. But everyone else was doing it, so it seemed justifiable.

The second thought was stronger: *He knows he gave you too much; he's testing you to see if you're honest.* I paused for a moment and decided to listen to the second thought. I took the extra $5 bill back to my boss and said, "Sir, you gave me five dollars too much."

Butch said, "Oh, thank you."

I went back to my register and worked the rest of the day. The next morning when I came to work, Butch called me into the office. He asked how I would feel about being promoted to manager. I accepted the position and became a manager that next day. To a seventeen-year-old kid, becoming a manager was like being on top of the world.

Wisdom gave me insight into the true nature of that situation. It let me in on my boss's secret. I knew I was being tested, and as a result of that information, I was able to make a decision that brought me promotion. Wisdom also helped me resist the temptation to keep the extra money. When I returned it, wisdom showed me that honesty has benefits attached.

Wisdom will give you special insight into the true nature of things, too. It will enable you to make decisions that result in the best outcome.

More Whispers from God

True wisdom will always guide you to govern yourself according to God's wisdom. I am convinced that the Lord wants to give His children this kind of wisdom. It is available for us. Can you imagine if wisdom was available to you on your job? What would the outcome be if you began to receive consistent wisdom into the true nature of things in your place of employment? Think of how you could advance if you had insight into the plans of those in upper-level management. What if they were planning something that would negatively affect you, and you had insight into it through wisdom? What could happen if envious employees set a trap for you and wisdom informed you?

Wisdom can also assist you proactively. It can help you solve the perplexing problems in your industry. With wisdom, you can receive insight as to how your company can profit more and increase the morale of its employees. You must believe that God can grant wisdom about how to do things better.

How about wisdom for parenting? What if each time your children tried to pull one over on you, you had insight into the true nature of what was going on? How much more effectively could you parent?

If you are an engineer or an inventor, this kind of wisdom would be invaluable. God can unlock secrets that would give you insight and understanding to solve perplexing problems and come up with new techniques.

Students must have this wisdom, too. Imagine the ability to have insight into the way your instructor thinks. That could help you know exactly how to study for tests or present projects.

Pastors and church leaders need this kind of wisdom. In order to grow strong churches and impact our communities, we must have true insight into the nature of people, places and things. Wisdom provides that.

I find my own desire for wisdom increasing. The more I think about its abilities, the more I crave it. I *must* have more wisdom. How about you? I have a feeling that God is ready to give us more wisdom, so let's keep learning more about it. I encourage you to pray regularly for the Spirit of wisdom and revelation (see Ephesians 1:17). God is eager to give it to us, if we just ask Him for it.

Decree to Receive Revelation

Lord, let Your Spirit of revelation rest on me. Reveal Your splendor and majesty. Let Your Spirit stretch upon me like a tent. Let me know the intricate details of my life and what You have for me to do. I decree that the same way Your hands formed the dry land, so I, too, will form things in the palm of my hands. I decree that You will reveal secrets to me and give me insight to make decisions. I decree that I have the answer to the question and the solution to the problem. You said for us to call to You and You will show us great and unsearchable things we do not know. My God, do not be silent or far off from me! Let those things be revealed to me now. I decree that my ears are open to hear from You. It is done in Jesus' name, Amen.

QUESTIONS FOR MEDITATION

1. Sometimes God presents His wisdom to us in revelation. For us, it often comes in that "Aha!" moment when understanding becomes clear to us. Think back

to one occasion when God gave you an "Aha!" moment. Did you recognize God's will in that moment? Did you thank God for the blessing of wisdom and revelation? The next time you recognize that God is giving you wisdom, be sure to thank Him.

2. Discernment and recognition are both parts of wisdom. When we face a problem, many times wisdom is clueing us in on how to solve it. We just have to recognize the clues and discern the information. Think of a tough problem you face right now. Are possible clues to a solution right there in front of you? Do you have yet to recognize them?

3. Most everybody has an "Aha!" moment now and then. Ask someone you are close to when the last time was that he or she had that kind of moment. What was the situation? What was the problem? How did God provide revelation? Did he or she recognize God's wisdom at that moment?

PRACTICAL TIPS

1. Reread 1 Kings 10:1–3 about Solomon. Memorize and get into your heart the passages where you see Solomon recognizing wisdom's whisper, understanding the truth and receiving wisdom's discernment to make the right decision. See if you can apply that same type of discernment in your life.

2. Continue to read and memorize wisdom quotes and literature. Continue to read (or reread) Proverbs, Ecclesiastes and Song of Songs. Saturate your mind with

wisdom daily, and make notes as to how wisdom reveals itself to you as you read.

3. To receive insight, we consistently must be listening. We must take every opportunity to hear God's voice through the Word of God, through books, through circumstances and through our open hearts. Make yourself a few signs that say, "Wisdom Waits." Place these in strategic spots where they will remind you to create a place for God's insight to come to you. For example, you might want to place one in your bedroom and pray for wisdom as you get ready to sleep. You might want to place another on the visor in your car or by your computer.

4

Knowledge

Wisdom's Brilliance

Knowledge is flour, but wisdom is bread.

—Austin O'Malley

I was not sure if I should go or not. I knew the conference would be huge, with thousands in attendance, and I did not want to get lost in the crowd. I desired a smaller setting that would lend itself to more personal attention. Another issue I had was the theme—leadership—a topic that was not uppermost in my mind. For years I thought prayer and the Word of God were all I needed.

To my detriment, I did not realize the value of learning about principles from a variety of sources. I had heard a few of John Maxwell's leadership messages, however, and admittedly they were beneficial. Since his company, INJOY, was hosting this conference, I decided to go in spite of my concerns. Before leaving I prayed, *God, let something happen at this conference that will change my life. Let me meet some-one there who will impact me greatly.*

By the end of the first day, I surmised that the conference was definitely beneficial. I went to my hotel room happy, contemplating what my next steps would be. The second morning, I ran into a young man seemingly by accident. He stretched out his hand and said, "Hi, I'm Kevin Small." We chatted for a few minutes about little things. He then asked how I liked the conference. His question was not posed like that of a regular attendee, though. He spoke as if he owned the place. His tone prompted me to ask what he did for a living. His reply: "I'm the president of INJOY."

Here was the head of the company right in front of me! Suddenly, I began to realize this was an opportunity standing before me. After a moment of wrestling with the possibility of being presumptuous, I said, "Kevin, I want to grow as a leader. Is there any possibility that if I have a question or two in the future, I could contact you?"

Kevin emphatically agreed, and he surprised me even more by saying that he would be happy to mentor me. I could not believe my ears. He then gave me a few guidelines regarding how the process would work. I walked away from the meeting with a new mentor—not just any mentor, but the president of a cutting-edge leadership organization owned by John Maxwell.

Kevin kept his word. We went to pro ball games and shared several dinners. Whenever I needed him, he made time for me. I only met with Kevin five or six times, but those sessions had a big impact on me. He seemed to get so much done during a day—a skill I significantly lacked. What he shared with me changed my life and the lives of many others.

Kevin taught me the concept of developing a life plan. He had planned out his entire life to the point of estimating the number of days he might yet have to live. He had calculated that if he lived to be ninety, he would have over twenty thousand days left on this planet. He did not want to waste a day, so he planned what he would accomplish during those days in the following areas: spiritual, financial, personal growth, family, ministry, career, self-development, health and fun.

This life plan concept lines up with Psalm 90:12, a prayer for God to "Teach us to number our days aright, that we may gain a heart of wisdom." This is exactly what Kevin did as he showed me a sample of his plan.

I was in awe. "Kevin, you're a genius," I said.

His reply: "No, Kyle, I learned this from someone else." He shocked me by telling me that almost nothing he does is original. He learns most of it from other people.

The concept of having a life plan changed my life. I have since developed my own plan of what I must accomplish in the areas in which I want to excel. I have counted and considered my days to incline my heart to wisdom, and my life is better because of it. By the way, one of the items on my life plan is to publish a book with a mainstream publisher. You are reading the fruit of that plan.

My experience with Kevin taught me a valuable lesson. If I want to incline my heart to wisdom, I must give time and energy to the pursuit. Put another way, if I want to know more, I must seek it out. In the rest of this chapter, we will learn about the steps we can take to develop our natural skills further. Although we are each born with various gifts and talents, we must discover what those are and consistently add to our skill level. This is wisdom.

Natural Gifts and Talents

The Master Creator demonstrates His wisdom through the natural gifts and talents He gives each of us. We see this clearly illustrated when God spoke to Moses about His provision for the building of the Tabernacle in the wilderness:

> See, I have chosen Bezalel son of Uri, the son of Hur, of the tribe of Judah, and *I have filled him with the Spirit of God, with skill, ability and knowledge in all kinds of crafts—to make artistic designs for work in gold, silver and bronze, to cut and set stones, to work in wood, and to engage in all kinds of craftsmanship.* Moreover, I have appointed Oholiab son of Ahisamach, of the tribe of Dan, to help him. Also I have given skill to all the craftsmen to make everything I have commanded you.
>
> Exodus 31:1–6, emphasis added

God gave the children of Israel the tall task of building a portable sanctuary in the barren desert. It needed to be practical, but designed according to a heavenly pattern. Israel had just been delivered from hundreds of years of slavery in Egypt. During their enslavement they built cities for Pharaoh, but that earthly architectural skill was not enough to equip them to build for the Master Architect. God instructed Moses, "Have them make a sanctuary for me, and I will dwell among them. Make this tabernacle and all its furnishings exactly like the pattern I will show you" (Exodus 25:8–9).

The requirements for the Tabernacle were so specific that they required men and women with specialized skills. God already chose certain ones, filled them with the Spirit and gave them wisdom. Their wisdom manifested as the ability to build to God's exact requirements. Scripture makes no mention of the people being trained for this kind of work. We are simply told that He filled them with the Spirit and with wisdom, enabling them to construct the Tabernacle according to His specifications.

Diversity Displays God's Wisdom

Have you ever been amazed by a young child with an innate ability that seems God-given, since it was obviously not passed down by a parent? My friend's little son has the ability to build things. No one knows where it came from because his dad cannot build a thing, yet the son is amazing. Watching what he can create with a set of blocks is astounding. All we can conclude is that God gave him a special gift. Perhaps we should call it "wisdom to build."

Even when our gifts reflect family interests, we can still marvel at the diversity of children who are in the same family with the same parents, yet have completely different personalities and talents. My siblings and I are no exception. The four of us represent unique talents. Kim, the oldest, is highly gifted intellectually. I am gifted with communication. Karen, my younger sister, is the most compassionate personality you will ever meet. She is a nurse. Kevin, my younger brother, is gifted in sports. We all grew up in the same house, seeing and hearing the same things, but our gifts, personalities and talents are all distinct. We are all crafted for a purpose, which should result in a degree of contentment with who we are. We must learn to rejoice in our uniqueness and not desire to be like others.

Some amazing people on this planet exhibit unusual gifts. If we are not careful, we will want to emulate them. Take Scott Flansburg, who was nicknamed "The Human Calculator" by Regis Philbin because of his amazing ability to do mathematical calculations in his head. Scott is in the *Guinness Book of World Records* for adding the same number to itself more times in fifteen seconds than the average person can do with a calculator. Now that is skill! I have a math background, but I do not need to emulate Scott to find my place on earth.

Perhaps you might identify more with Feliks Zemdegs. He holds the world record for solving the 3x3 Rubik's Cube puzzle. His time is just 5.66 seconds. That is fast, especially considering that out of the hundreds of times I have tried to solve this cube, I have never succeeded. Should I rejoice with Feliks or envy him? I need to celebrate my innate characteristics and be grateful for his. This leaves no room for envy.

If you are musically inclined, you will love David Garrett's violin skill. He is the fastest in the world—able to play "Flight of the Bumblebee" in just 1 minute 6.56 seconds. These are unusual and impressive gifts that have been honed to an extraordinary degree. We must be careful not to wish that we had someone else's gift. Rather, we can—and should—discover our own gifts. Rejoice in discovering what you can do. Your natural gifts are God's wisdom given to you.

Discovering Your Natural Skill

Everybody is good at something. I have yet to meet somebody who does not have any skills at all. It may take time to discover your skill set, but I promise there exists a "pot of gold"—your destiny—at the end of your gift rainbow.

The Bible shares some amazing facts about what God mapped out for us before He created us. "In him we were also chosen, having been predestined according to the plan of him who works out everything in conformity with the purpose of his will" (Ephesians 1:11). We are all prescribed a destiny. The Greek word used for *predestine* in this verse is *prooridzo*. *Pro* in Greek is like our prefix *pre*, which means "before." *Oridzo* is where we get our word *horizon*. We have a horizon, a destination, a determination established by God before we arrive on this planet. We are not placed here by accident or happenstance. We are destined before we arrive, and our gift mix matches our destination. We are all given various "personality programming" by the Lord. This "pre-horizon" is not on automatic pilot. We must choose to cooperate with it, as we will see in the pages ahead.

Almost accidentally, I discovered a gift God gave me. I barely finished high school. My grade point average was the lowest D possible a student could get and still graduate. I finished the class of 1983 ranked an "impressive" 268 out of 280. I had no academic motivation, even though the brain-power existed in me to do better.

The summer after I graduated, I had a change of mind. I decided to make something of myself. I enrolled as a full-time student at Alabama State University. It was something of a miracle that I was accepted, considering my poor grade point average. True to the promise I made myself, I worked hard and made good grades. One of my classes, however, proved daunting. As much as I determined to do well, precalculus class wore me out. My poor performance became a source of frustration.

One night when homework got the best of me, I closed my precalculus book and resolved to give up and drop out of the class. In my frustration, I sat for a few minutes staring at the yellow textbook with red writing. I noticed how thick it was. I opened it again, flipping through the pages from beginning to end, looking at the massive assortment of complex equations and variables. Then, in a moment, my perspective changed. I uttered these words out loud: "If someone is smart enough to write this stuff, I know I am at least smart enough to learn it."

I opened the book again, determined to master the subject. This choice became more than self-talk. It became a landmark in making a course correction in my destiny. I did so well in precalculus that at the end of the semester, my instructor said, "You have a gift for math; you should major in it." Today I have a B.A. in math and a master's degree in math education.

I have a gift from God to think logically and linearly by nature—but I was not aware of that gift until I struggled with a subject that logically, I should have handled easily. The gift already resided within me, yet I had to work at precalculus to better myself. Through the experience of sweat and near defeat, I became aware of my natural gifting. Precalculus, my nemesis, became my hero.

This story demonstrates how wisdom can become as brilliant as a diamond. Life experiences cut the piece of rough rock that we are into a beautiful gem. Applying wisdom to our lives polishes the diamond until it shines brightly for others to see. Many of us possess untapped hidden treasures. God uses a wide variety of ways to help us discover these. Let's pause and pray for the ability to better discern the gifts wisdom has given us.

Prayer for Discerning Our Gifts

Heavenly Father, I ask in the name of Jesus that You open my eyes and allow me to see how wisdom has uniquely gifted me. Expose the areas in which wisdom exists in my life, even if it is in seed form. Uncover hidden talents and resources Your wisdom has planted in me. Grant me the boldness to cooperate with wisdom in all my skills. Help me be a better steward of that which You have given me. In Jesus' name, Amen.

Enhancing Your Wisdom

Natural skill is a gift from God, but not a finite one. No matter what level of wisdom or gifting you have from birth, you can increase it. Natural skill grows through experience. I am sure you realize that the older we get, the wiser we typically become. Life's experiences add to and polish our natural skill, resulting in more wisdom in our gifted areas. Wisdom grows out of a combination of learning and experience over a period of time.

I played the trumpet for many years. The longer I played and the more I practiced, the more my wisdom grew about how to play better, longer, stronger and with a good tone. I learned tricks for playing in cold weather and what to do when my lips became tired. Wisdom emerged as a result of skill plus experience. This enhancement was not caused by wisdom from above, but by physical effort used to increase my knowledge, gifting and ability.

At times we allow our attitude to hinder growth in our gifts. The wrong attitude can limit us, causing us to feel unqualified for a specific task. When this happens, we place a lid on our lives that caps our potential. I nearly did that when I thought about dropping precalculus because of my frustration. If I had given up, who knows when I might have uncovered my gifting in that area—if ever. But when we couple our instinctive gifts and talents with methods to improve them, the result is greater wisdom. This is an important principle. No matter how gifted we are, we must always seek improvement. A little wisdom can become great wisdom, and greater wisdom can become even greater.

Increasing Your Practical Skills

We must improve every gift God has given us. We are stewards of these gifts and ought to improve them. Thomas Edison agreed when he said, "Genius is one percent inspiration and ninety-nine percent perspiration."[1]

Becoming a genius sounds like a lot of work! Yet God appreciates it when we add to the talents He has given us. Jesus shared a parable that illustrates this perfectly. In His story, three servants received bags of gold from their master before he went on a long journey. "To one he gave five bags of gold, to another two bags, and to another one bag, each according to his ability" (Matthew 25:15, NIV2010). Even though the master in this parable left no specific instructions, "The man who had received five bags of gold went at once and put his money to work and gained five bags more. So also, the one with two bags of gold gained two more" (verses 16–17). These two servants found a way to double what they had been given. Notice each servant was given a portion "according to his ability."

This parable shows how God entrusts us with our natural gifts. Some may be given a gift that will get them to the third round of *American Idol*, and some are gifted enough to win. Many are gifted to play basketball, but there are not many Michael Jordans on this planet. In the parable, two of the servants, regardless of their portion, doubled what they had. Let's face it—all we can work with is what we have. Thank God we can make what we have better.

The servant who only received one bag of gold proved himself a little different. He "dug a hole in the ground and hid his master's money" (verse 18). Satisfied with the status quo, he did not even try to improve on what he was given. Mr. One Bagger's real motivation was fear. When his master returned to take account of his stewardship, the servant's excuse was, "I knew that you are a hard man, harvesting where you have not sown and gathering where you have not scattered seed. So I was afraid and went out and hid your gold in the ground. See, here is what belongs to you" (verses 24–25).

Mr. One Bagger received pretty strict punishment. The master took the one bag he had determined to protect out of fear and gave it to the servant who now had ten. Perhaps this is where the saying "use it or lose it" comes from. I wonder how many times I have cheated myself out of more experiential wisdom due to fear of failure. Perhaps like me, you can think of a time or two in your life when you should have done something that would have greatly enhanced your abilities, but you did not do it.

We cannot change the past, but we can decide to go forward and do whatever is necessary to improve our gifts, thereby increasing wisdom. Let's use and improve on our gifts. I want to give you some suggestions about things to look at that may help you on your journey. First, let's make a decree about maximizing our gifts.

Decree for Growing in Wisdom in our Gifting

I decree that I will not be lazy or lethargic in using and improving what God has given me. With God's grace, I will make every effort to become polished in my area of giftedness. I will not only give God back the exact amount of gifting He gave me; I will grow and improve with His help. In Jesus' name, Amen.

Assessing Your Growth

Knowledge and experience are obviously beneficial when it comes to increasing our skills. However, most of us need to be challenged to press our gifts forward. I want to ask three questions that will help you assess whether you have positioned yourself to keep pressing your gifts toward the mark God has set for you.

What Are You Reading?

The first way to grow in knowledge is by reading. Think about it: A person can spend fifty years of his or her life learning the best way to do something, and then write a book on it. That allows you and me to process in a few days the wisdom it took the author fifty years to gather. And what did it cost? Maybe $19.99 and a few hours out of our day—not bad for the benefit we receive. Within the pages of a book, we often gain more than pure knowledge. We learn from the experience of another person. Even if the book costs more than twenty bucks, what value should we place on the author's years of experience? In this day of electronic media that increasingly competes to prevent us from getting lost in a good book, we should devise a plan to regularly read books that enhance our natural gifting.

I recently was asked to help an organization solve a few problems. When I arrived, I was able to see the challenges they faced right off. I had a solution because I had read about it in a book a few weeks before. They thought I was ultrasmart and possessed incredible wisdom. I did have wisdom—wisdom I learned from the author of the book I had just read. I shared the book with the leader of the organization, and now he is wiser, too.

What Are You Asking?

The second way to add to your natural gifts and grow your wisdom is by asking questions. Questions never asked are questions never answered. However, many people are too timid to ask questions, lest they be judged for not knowing something. Asking questions is a prerequisite to discovery. Many biblical doctrines are based on responses to questions asked in Scripture. One of my favorite examples is in Matthew 24 and 25. These two chapters list critically important end-time events. Jesus taught about them in response to a question the disciples asked. "Tell us," they said, "when will this happen, and what will be the sign of your coming and of the end of the age?" (Matthew 24:3). Had the disciples not queried Jesus, we may not have had available the vital information about how to position ourselves before God in these last times.

Have you ever been lost and had to ask for directions? If you are lost, you do not know where you are or how to get to where you want to go. Why do some men have a hard time asking for directions? Perhaps because it forces them to admit weakness—the weakness of not knowing something as simple as where they are. The same is true in life; somebody knows what you need to do to get where you want to go, and sometimes you need to ask for that information. Somebody has a solution that can help you solve your family problem or financial problem. It does not matter if the question is how to lose weight or how to play checkers better. Somebody can help you, and more than likely they are willing.

After being married long enough for my wife to observe me in social settings, she asked me a question: "Why is it that when we get around other people, you don't talk much—you just ask a lot of questions?"

My answer to her was, "Honey, I want to learn. If all I do is talk, then I will never learn what they know."

I have learned that when you ask questions politely and sincerely, more times than not you will get more information than you needed. This is especially true if you are grateful for the response and let the person know it.

Who Is Giving You Counsel?

A third way to grow in knowledge is by seeking mentors and counselors. No matter how brilliant or gifted people are, they will always need counsel. Proverbs 15:22 says, "Plans fail for lack of counsel, but with many advisers they succeed." We must both seek out capable mentors/counselors and learn to recognize wise counsel when it is given.

The story of Moses leading the children of Israel through the wilderness sealed for me my eternal need for good counsel.

85

Bible scholars estimate the crowd that left Egypt at about three million people. God was so close to His people that He showed Himself in a pillar of cloud by day and a pillar of fire by night. God was so close to Moses that "the LORD would speak to Moses face to face, as a man speaks with his friend" (Exodus 33:11). God Himself testified of Moses' special relationship with Him:

> When a prophet of the LORD is among you,
> I reveal myself to him in visions,
> I speak to him in dreams.
> But this is not true of my servant Moses;
> he is faithful in all my house.
> With him I speak face to face,
> clearly and not in riddles;
> he sees the form of the LORD.
> Why then were you not afraid
> to speak against my servant Moses?
>
> Numbers 12:6–8

One might assume that a man with such an invitation from God would need no counsel. He should know what to do in every circumstance. And if a baffling situation arose, all Moses would need to do was ask God, since he had the face-to-face thing going on. But that was not the case. Moses made an unwise decision regarding how to structure his ministry. His father-in-law, Jethro, came to visit and saw that Moses was the only judge for three million people. People would line up all day long to bring issues directly to Moses for a verdict. When Jethro saw this out-of-control situation, he advised Moses, "What you are doing is not good. You and these people who come to you will only wear yourselves out. The work is too heavy for you; you cannot handle it alone. Listen now to me and I will give you some advice"

(Exodus 18:17–19). Then Jethro told Moses to select leaders over the people and have them rule on all but the most difficult issues, sharing the load with Moses. "If you do this and God so commands," Jethro said, "you will be able to stand the strain, and all these people will go home satisfied" (verse 23).

Good counsel is invaluable. Moses became a more effective leader by heeding Jethro's wise advice. The mentorship and counsel I received through Kevin from INJOY is still bearing fruit some ten-plus years later.

Intentional Improvement

These questions are a few checkpoints that can aid us in knowing how to regularly add wisdom to our natural abilities. As you answer and act on them, my prayer is that you will see great increase. One lesson wisdom has taught me is that growth happens intentionally. If we are going to improve our natural abilities, it will be because we do it on purpose. Atrophy is one law that seems consistent among human beings. We must work hard to keep in shape. Ask anybody who has a gym membership—staying in shape is hard work.

I am grateful for every natural grace on my life, but I also hunger to grow and gain more. Wisdom has taught me much about how my attitude affects the percentage of wise and foolish choices I make. The next chapter will give you some powerful tools with which to implement an attitude adjustment, no matter how "well-adjusted" you are.

But first, let's look at some questions and practical tips that will shine a light on where we are as far as identifying and developing our natural gifts through knowledge and experience. Wisdom is but a few choices away.

QUESTIONS FOR MEDITATION

1. Identify your gifts and talents and write them down. Be as specific as possible. Some may seem minor to you, but include them. Look at your list and circle the top one or ones that describe your passion or make you feel fulfilled. Take time to praise God for your entire list, but ask Him to stimulate the top talents you have and give you a picture of the destiny He has for these gifts.

2. Ask yourself the three questions mentioned in the text to assess where you are in your journey in terms of your top passion(s): What have you read, or what are you currently reading to challenge you to press forward in your gifts? Are you easily able to ask questions in your field of expertise when someone who is also an expert crosses your path? Are you in a mentorship situation with someone who has skills and experience beyond yours?

3. Set a growth goal for the areas in your life that you seek to improve. Make the goal practical, with specific and measurable targets. Then list steps you will take to achieve the goal. Develop an accountability partner to walk the path of growth with you. You never know when you might need a bit of encouragement along the way.

PRACTICAL TIPS

Reading

- Read a variety of books. Do not settle for just one type of fiction or nonfiction title. Choose biographies, articles, textbooks, self-help books and many others. Expose yourself to different materials. You will be better as a result.

- Map out a reading plan. Choose which books you will read in a given year.
- Schedule reading times in your day and week. Plan times when you steal away just to read. Go to a park or your favorite place in the house. Get away from stressors and consider it "me time."
- Stop, pause and pray. When something impacts you in a book, pause for a moment and pray/meditate on it. This allows new principles you discover to assimilate more fully into your life.

Mentoring

- Make sure you seek counsel from people of good character whom you trust. More than asking if somebody offers good information, you should ask if he or she is a person of good character. When people do not have enough character to follow their own advice, you probably should not be listening to what they have to say. By their fruit you shall know them. Check out their relationships, personalities and references. Make sure you feel really comfortable in your insides when you are with them. If you have some negative feelings, you should probably obey them.
- Seek counsel/mentorship from successful people.
- Find a counselor with good listening skills. Successful counselors listen more than they speak. If you run into someone who is more interested in sharing his or her knowledge than in hearing your hurts, that person is not your mentor or counselor.
- Seek a counselor who will not judge you. Counselors and mentors should not belittle you; they should build you

up. You should receive clarity and hope from a mentoring session.

- Seek a counselor who will tell you the truth even if it hurts. You also need a counselor who will speak the truth in love.

5

Attitude

A Glass Half-Full of Wisdom

Attitude is a little thing that makes a big difference.

—Winston Churchill

I understood culture shock. Having grown up in New York City before I moved to the small town of Tuskegee, Alabama, caused me to be well acquainted with what it feels like to be different. I was thirteen when we moved to Tuskegee—just the age when friends and peer pressure are most important in a young teen's life. It took me a while to get over people laughing at me every time I spoke because I "talked funny." To me, my northeast speech was not a car wreck—it was just a little accident. After all, what was wrong with me drinking *soda* while the local kids drank *pop*? I called the one who gave birth to me *Mother*, not *Mama*, and dads were called

Father. These and a myriad of other differences brought me constant ridicule. Eventually folks got used to me and I got used to them. I shifted my New York accent a bit to blend in so that I could be understood. After all, I was outnumbered.

Perhaps it was these experiences that prepared me for the first day of my tenth-grade year in high school. The entire student body of several hundred kids milled outside, waiting for the school doors to open. The parking lot was almost as loud as an indoor pro football game. Friends got reacquainted for the first time in months. The teachers were inside preparing for classes, so our outside activities were unregulated. Talk about rancor—it was a mess. Suddenly, a large green Buick pulled into the parking lot. The driver stopped the car right in front of the door where the largest crowd was gathered. A few students glanced up, but at this point they did not pay too much attention. That quickly changed when the back doors of the car opened and two white kids, a brother and sister, stepped out. Tuskegee Institute High School was an all-black school, so a drastic hush swept over the crowd. Everyone froze in their tracks, stopped talking and stared at these two white kids for what seemed like an eternity. The outsiders looked like deer caught in the headlights, paralyzed with fear, not knowing what to do.

Without giving it much thought I stepped out of the crowd, walked over to the boy and said, "Hi, I'm Kyle Searcy. Welcome to Tuskegee Institute High School." Immediately the boy's flushed face changed to a more pleasant demeanor. His fear subsided, and he introduced his sister. As I became acquainted with Collin and Carrie, their dad drove off feeling comfortable that his kids would be fine. The crowd slowly went back to their activities, seeming to accept that these kids must be all right. Collin remains a good friend of mine to this day. He often reminds me that my gesture was an oasis in the desert. He had felt petrified and was ready to jump back into the car and tell his dad to drive off as fast as he could. The incident with Collin and Carrie reminds me constantly that one act of kindness can go a long way in almost any situation or even in changing one's life. Kindness is an attitude—an attitude that wisdom embraces.

Wisdom's Altitude Is Attitude

I am an instrument-rated pilot. Whenever I am flying in the clouds, my most important flight instrument is the altitude indicator. Some call it the artificial horizon. This instrument shows how my aircraft is positioned relative to the horizon. If the little artificial airplane on my instrument is above the horizon bar, I am ascending. If it is below the bar, I am descending. It is the same thing with our attitude in life.

Wisdom has taught me how a positive, faith-filled, optimistic attitude will cause me to maximize life and get the best out of most situations. In this chapter we will explore how wisdom, if we defer to it, will navigate us toward an optimistic outlook and a pleasant demeanor. We will also see how a negative outlook produces the opposite. Wisdom, when we yield to it, delivers the best possible outcome in any situation. Our attitudes are not excluded from this condition. Wisdom applied to our temperament will result in an optimistic outlook. The more we embrace wisdom's teaching and the more we learn about it, the more virtues will be formed in our life.

Everyone wants a more positive attitude. If you lined up one hundred random people and interviewed each by asking, "Would you like to have a more positive outlook and a more pleasant demeanor?" virtually all of them would answer yes. Even those who think they already have it together would not mind a little more optimism. Wisdom will always lead us toward the positive side. If we follow its trail, we will end up in the promised land of a hopeful outlook and a Christlike persona.

I am not speaking of perfection. We are all tempted at times to have a bad moment or a bad day—we are flawed human beings. I am talking about developing the ability to see the good in situations much more than the bad. Wisdom will show us how to avoid the trap of pessimistic living, which can be costly to our emotional well-being.

A perfect example of how a bad attitude can thwart a desired outcome is when the children of Israel were ready to enter the Promised Land. This was the culmination of a very long, very horrible, yet very miraculous quest. Israel had been enslaved in Egypt for 430 years. During those arduous years, they prayed and cried for freedom. Finally, God sent Moses and freed them through powerful signs and wonders. Daily, these people watched impossible things happen in which God showed His superior power over the pharaoh and the gods of Egypt.

To the Israelites, the ten plagues were more than a list from the Bible. They experienced firsthand the outcry of their captors when the Egyptians suffered the plagues of insects (flies, locusts and lice), environmental disasters (water to blood, darkness and fiery hail) and finally death (of livestock and the firstborn). The plagues' effects produced a distinct difference between the "plagued and the plagued-nots." Israel remained immune to the harmful conditions, one after another (see Exodus 7:14–12:36).

When the children of Israel finally left Egypt, the country was destroyed. Not much was left. In fact, the Egyptians were so tired of the situation, they piled precious jewels, gold and other treasures on the Israelites . . . almost paying just to get rid of them. What an exit! If there were ever any folks who should have embraced enough wisdom to maintain a positive attitude, it should have been this group of rescued people.

Once released, Israel escaped ambush by miraculously walking through the Red Sea. The very waters they so feared drowned the Egyptian army right before their eyes. This kind of powerful display should have resulted in eternal gratitude and unwavering faith. If Israel allowed wisdom to speak to them and teach them, they would have walked in a tremendous spirit of gratitude. They should have exemplified David's future words:

> Preserve sound judgment and discernment,
>   do not let them out of your sight;
> they will be life for you,
>   an ornament to grace your neck.
> Then you will go on your way in safety,
>   and your foot will not stumble;
> when you lie down, you will not be afraid;
>   when you lie down, your sleep will be sweet.
> Have no fear of sudden disaster
>   or of the ruin that overtakes the wicked,
> for the LORD will be your confidence
>   and will keep your foot from being snared.
>
> Proverbs 3:21–26

God's faithfulness continued. He delighted in bringing Israel to the land of promise, although they encountered a few tests along the way. Their response was far less positive than expected. They murmured and complained, at times verbally expressing a desire to go back to slavery in Egypt.

In an effort to build their faith, Moses sent twelve spies to the land of promise. He admonished the spies to gather some important information:

"See what the land is like and whether the people who live there are strong or weak, few or many. What kind of land do they live in? Is it good or bad? What kind of towns do they live in? Are they unwalled or fortified? How is the soil? Is it fertile or poor? Are there trees on it or not? Do your best to bring back some of the fruit of the land."

Numbers 13:18–20

This foray was designed to provide major encouragement to the people. After hearing about the beauty of the land and viewing some of its produce, they would be motivated to go forth into their destiny—or at least that was what Moses hoped. The spies explored the land for forty days. They returned with just one cluster of grapes so large that two of them had to carry it on a pole (see Numbers 13:23). All Israel gathered to hear about the spies' faith-building, exploratory journey. Instead of building faith, however, most of the men who had gone in said, "We can't attack those people; they are stronger than we are. . . . The land we explored devours those living in it. All the people we saw there are of great size. . . . We seemed like grasshoppers in our own eyes, and we looked the same to them" (verses 31–33).

When the masses heard the negative report, they grumbled and wept, denouncing their God and Moses. They strategized about finding a new leader to take them back into Egypt instead of going into the land they were promised. Needless to say, God was upset. His verdict:

> "Not one of the men who saw my glory and the miraculous signs I performed in Egypt and in the desert but who disobeyed me and tested me ten times—not one of them will ever see the land I promised on oath to their forefathers. No one who has treated me with contempt will ever see it."

Numbers 14:22–23

This crowd forfeited their destiny because of a bad attitude. They failed to allow wisdom to help them see the glass as half-full rather than half-empty. Only two of the spies, Caleb and

Joshua, were allowed to enter the Promised Land. Why? They had "a different spirit," a wise spirit that caused them to see the promise of God as greater than their problems (Numbers 14:24).

If you were to chart out the miracles and keeping power of God on behalf of the Israelites and their corresponding negative attitude, the result would be a sorry sight indeed. We may like to point the finger at these exasperating people, but how do we fare in similar situations? What is our attitude like when we have more month left over than we have money? How do we respond to delayed answers to prayer? How do we react to trials and unexplained difficulties? If we follow wisdom's path, we look at the potential offered in a situation, not the problem.

Prayer to Choose Wisdom's Path

Father, I ask in the name of Jesus that You help me see through wisdom's eyes. Grace me to see more possibilities than problems and more opportunities than obstacles. Help me not to yield to the temptation toward a negative outlook. Help me especially to see Your track record of faithfulness in my life. Help me not to doubt Your promises. Thank You for hearing my prayer. In Jesus' name, Amen.

Wisdom Creates a Proper Attitude

We cannot underestimate the power of our attitude in determining our outcome in life. Winston Churchill spoke this truth: "Attitude is a little thing that makes a big difference." Napoleon Hill, in his thought-provoking book *Success through a Positive Mental Attitude*, wrote,

> When Henley wrote the poetic lines, "I am the master of my fate, I am the captain of my soul," he could have informed us that we are the masters of our fate because we are masters

first, of our attitudes. Our attitudes shape our future. This is a universal law.[1]

I would like to go a step further and say this is a universal law that is irreversible.

Mildred Searcy is the greatest philosopher who ever walked this planet as far as I am concerned—she also happens to have been my mom. She would always say this about attitude: "What goes around comes back around. The way you are toward life and others will come back to you." She was right. I have witnessed this principle time and again in my life. The Bible confirms my mom's wisdom when it discusses the power of our inner disposition becoming reality. Proverbs, the wisdom book, says in beautiful King James English, "As [a man] thinketh in his heart, so is he" (Proverbs 23:7, KJV). I am sure it is thoughts like these that caused the gold medal skater Scott Hamilton to remark, "The only disability in life is a bad attitude."[2]

As important as attitude is, it is more important to know that God does not predetermine our attitudes—we choose them. Philippians 2:5 says, "Your attitude should be the same as that of Christ Jesus." How could Scripture encourage us to have a certain attitude if we were powerless to choose what our attitude would be? There would be no wisdom in that. Our attitudes can never become new if we do not tune them to wisdom's standard for a proper attitude: "You were taught . . . to be made new in the attitude of your minds; and to put on the new self, created to be like God in true righteousness and holiness" (Ephesians 4:22–24).

The God of Wisdom

God is wise. There is no foolishness in or about Him. Romans 16:27 tells us He is called "the only wise God." Jesus, as part of the Godhead, is therefore also wise. A few thousand years ago, Isaiah prophesied of the coming Messiah, who would be of the lineage of King David. He describes the Spirit of Messiah as possessing the sevenfold Spirit of the Lord. Can you guess what comes early in Isaiah's list?

> A shoot will come up from the stump of Jesse;
> from his roots a Branch will bear fruit.
> The Spirit of the LORD will rest on him—
> *the Spirit of wisdom and of understanding,*
> the Spirit of counsel and of power,
> the Spirit of knowledge and of the fear of the LORD.
>
> Isaiah 11:1–2, emphasis added

Seven attributes adequately describe the character and nature of Jesus in His earthly ministry. One of them is the "Spirit of wisdom." You cannot separate wisdom from Christ. He both *contains* wisdom and *is* wisdom. Colossians 2:2–3 makes it plain, declaring that in Christ "are hidden all the treasures of wisdom and knowledge." This passage touches me. I have discovered through years of reading the Bible that each word used by the writers of Scripture is intentional. When Scripture uses the word *all*, it means each and every one; nothing is left outside when the word *all* is used. It does not matter if the language is Greek, Hebrew or Aramaic, *all* means *all*. *All* of the treasures of wisdom and knowledge are hidden in our Lord and Savior, King Jesus. A treasure is a place valuables are stored or hidden. The value of *all* wisdom and *all* knowledge is hidden in Christ. Unbelievable? No, it *is* believable! Let's take a moment to pray for the revelation of wisdom that resides in Christ.

Prayer to Know Jesus Christ as Wisdom

Father, I thank You that as I fellowship with the Lord Jesus, more wisdom is revealed to me and in me. Thank You for revealing through Jesus the depth of Your wisdom for every area of my life. Whenever I face a challenging situation, I will remember how Jesus has been made wisdom for me. I declare that I have the mind of Christ, which is the fullness of wisdom. I choose to dwell in Him and He in me—therefore I am never without wisdom! In Jesus' name, Amen.

God's Wise Attitude

Since God is wisdom, what attributes does His attitude display? How has His wisdom presented itself? Are there any biblical clues to the demeanor God chooses? There certainly are—they are called the fruit of the Spirit. Do you want to know what God's personality is like? Look at the fruit or products of His Spirit. "But the fruit of the Spirit is love, joy, peace, patience, kindness, goodness, faithfulness, gentleness, and self-control" (Galatians 5:22–23).

God could choose any persona He desired. The Creator of all things could have chosen a myriad of ways to represent Himself, but He chose these traits. In a sense, they could be called the "fruit of wisdom" since God, in His wisdom, chose them. All of these wonderful traits represent a positive mental attitude, but they also represent responses and the demeanor wisdom encourages us to embrace. It makes sense that "the only wise God" would embrace a wise way to live. But God does not stop there. The good news is that God also seeks to form these traits in us. The Spirit of God works tirelessly to manifest this fruit in our lives. Let's briefly look at each one:

Love (*agape* in Greek)—self-sacrificing, unconditional, unwavering commitment

Joy (*chara* in Greek)—rejoicing and gladness

Peace (*eirene* in Greek)—tranquility of mind and harmony with others

Longsuffering (*makrothumía* in Greek)—to restrain yourself before acting

Kindness (*christótos* in Greek)—usefulness

Goodness (*agathasúne* in Greek)—active benevolence

Faithfulness (*pístis* in Greek)—firm persuasion or conviction of the truth

Gentleness (*praótos* in Greek)—mildness, forbearance

Self-control (*egkráteia* in Greek)—continence, temperance

Now that we have looked at these fruits, let's test wisdom's attitude preference. For a moment, imagine you are a company manager about to hire an employee. Mike, a middle-aged man, applies for the job. He impressed you in the interview, but you want to check what others who know him might say about him. You send out a request for a reference to his former employer, who reveals the following: "Mike has great patience with people; situations that frustrate most people do not seem to rattle him. I have known Mike for the last several years and have had the privilege of observing him in professional, family and religious settings. Mike exhibits a strong degree of self-sacrificing love. He is always upbeat, happy and usually displays a great deal of peace. He gets along very well with others. He is kind and actively caring toward those around him. Mike has integrity and deeply held convictions that produce a great work ethic. His faith certainly causes him to move the ball downfield when our team needs to score. Although he is a gentleman and meek in nature, he also exercises great self-control."

If you received such a reference, would you hire Mike? I would. What if someone like Mike proposed to you or your sister? Marriage would be a real consideration! In fact, I cannot think of many people or circumstances in which someone would not be drawn toward a person with an attitude such as Mike exudes. We should desire the same reputation!

What Dictates Our Attitude?

If we want to be wise, we need to learn to live our lives based on the reality wisdom reveals, not on circumstances. Wisdom helps us see that we cannot dictate our attitude and emotional state based on what happens. We have to take control of situations and see the positive in them. Wisdom helps us to do this, as the apostle James was well aware. He wrote,

> Consider it pure joy, my brothers, whenever you face trials of many kinds, because you know that the testing of your faith develops perseverance. Perseverance must finish its work so that you may be mature and complete, not lacking anything. If any of you lacks wisdom, he should ask God, who gives generously to all without finding fault, and it will be given to him.
>
> James 1:2–5

In these verses, James has an important lesson for us about attitude. We should choose pure joy when various hardships hit our lives. How can we do this? By knowing what they produce in us. Wisdom helps us see the benefit we can receive even from bad situations. With God's help, good can be produced from everything in this life. If we ever get into a circumstance in which we lack the wisdom to see any good in it, we must take James's advice. We should stop, ask God for wisdom and expect He will give it to us.

We might have our doubts as to whether this can apply to every situation we face, yet wisdom is available to change our attitude—even if we are in prison. Frederick Langbridge said,

"Two men look out from prison bars; one sees the mud, and one the stars."[3] Wisdom will help you see the stars instead of mud every time.

A few years ago, I was attending a pastors' prayer summit with several leaders when Doug Small, the facilitator, told the story of Pastor Clay, an underground mission's worker in China for thirty years. Nine of his thirty years were served under the oppressive Mao regime. Pastor Clay was eventually arrested for being a Christian and put in jail for eighteen years. During that time, he was commanded to work in the dung pit. His job was to go to all the jail cells and collect the buckets of human waste, dig a big hole and bury the dung. He would later go back and dig it up again to be used as fertilizer. The prisoners hated that job. It was considered the highest form of punishment. Many died of infectious disease after only a few months of working the dung pit, but Pastor Clay lasted nine years working that disdainful job. In fact, each time his turn was up, he actually volunteered to go back into the pit and work!

Pastor Clay has long since been released from prison and now resides in the United States. During an interview someone asked him, "What was the most significant and meaningful time you had while in China?"

Pastor Clay said it was the nine years he spent in the dung pit. The interviewer thought Pastor Clay must have misunderstood the question, so he repeated it. Pastor Clay answered the same way again, "The nine years I spent in the dung pit in prison was the best time of my service in China." He then explained that in China you were not allowed any open expressions of Christianity. You could not sing, pray or praise out loud, but since nobody wanted to go into the dung pit, Pastor Clay was always there alone and free to express his faith. Often covered from head to toe with dung, he would sing and praise God with all of his heart. There, surrounded by human waste, he enjoyed uninterrupted fellowship with God and experienced the best time of his life. When asked what his favorite song was to sing in the dung pit, he said it was the familiar hymn "In the Garden" by C. Austin Miles:

> I come to the garden alone
> While the dew is still on the roses
> And the voice I hear falling on my ear
> The Son of God discloses.
>
> And He walks with me, and He talks with me,
> And He tells me I am His own;
> And the joy we share as we tarry there,
> None other has ever known. . . .[4]

Wisdom can cause you to turn a dung-pit experience into a garden. Let's pray that we would have wisdom's eyesight.

Prayer for Wisdom's Eyesight

Father, I ask that You grant me wisdom in all the uncomfortable situations I currently face. Grant me grace, as You did with Pastor Clay, to see the best in every situation. Help me not to waste energy wallowing in self-pity. Cause me to realize at all times that I alone control my inward reality and choose my attitude. Help me to resist the negative pull toward a pessimistic outlook. Help me to see the stars whenever I peer out from underneath my problems. Thank You for hearing me, Lord. In Jesus' name, Amen.

Wisdom will cause our attitude to soar. It will lift us above the common, seemingly gravitational pull on humanity toward a negative outlook. If we take just a few steps in wisdom's direction, we will begin to see life from a different perspective. The first step we should take is to grow more love in our hearts for God. This alone has unappreciated transforming power. We will discuss this more in the next chapter, but first, let's put the principles from this chapter into action in our lives.

QUESTIONS FOR MEDITATION

1. In your opinion, how much of life is controlled by your attitude? Is it easier for you to see a glass as half-empty or half-full? Do you think the main cause of a negative attitude is wrong beliefs about life or certain aspects of it? How will seeing life through negative beliefs create an unhappy life or one that seems downright pointless?

2. What beliefs do you need to change in order to change your attitude? How will this change demonstrate wisdom in your future?

3. Is attitude merely positive thinking? Why or why not? Does being positive mean ignoring what is happening around you and living within some kind of "positive bubble"?

4. How does attitude tie into God's wisdom within a negative situation? What is the source of the power to keep a wholesome attitude for a week, a month or even nine years?

PRACTICAL TIPS

1. John Hagee said, "Paul never developed a negative attitude. He picked his bloody body up out of the dirt and

went back into the city where he had almost been stoned to death, and he said, 'Hey, about that sermon I didn't finish preaching—here it is!' "[5] Is there a situation you face in which it feels as though your emotions, your career or your relationships have been "stoned to death"? If not, you can be sure such a situation will come up in the future. Make a plan for creating an attitude check that brings purpose and wisdom to situations trying to convert you to negativism. If you develop a cache of Scripture verses, quotes and positive people to turn to, you can use this resource in the future.

2. Make a chart of negative situations you might face in the future and the attitude God would delight in you having in the midst of them. Also list Scripture verses that support a positive attitude and quotes from Christians whom you admire. Add the names of people you personally know who have faced some of the negative situations you wrote down, yet have not been negatively affected by them.

3. If we cannot change our past, cannot change how other people may act and cannot change the inevitable, we must learn to change what we are able to change—our attitude. What would you like to change about your attitude? Make a list and take these things to prayer each day for the next thirty days. Allow God to reveal His attitude as He bestows His wisdom on you.

6

Wisdom's First Commandment

"Love the Lord your God with all your heart
and with all your soul and with all your mind.
This is the first and greatest commandment."

—Matthew 22:37–38

It was a mild February afternoon. I was driving my old 1985 Chevy Spectrum the first time I said it, but I never realized how drastically my life would change by saying these few words: "God, if You are real, I will give my life to You completely." It was the beginning of a journey for me that will continue for eternity. My salvation experience meant so much to me that I immediately devoted myself to living for Him.

As I mentioned in chapter 3, I was a senior in college when I surrendered to Jesus. I immediately took inventory of every area of my life and presented it to God. I wanted to be sure He was pleased with everything. I presented my college fraternity to God, saying, "If You don't want me to be part of this fraternity, I'll get out." I was two months away from graduating with a mathematics degree when I prayed with a sincere heart, "God, if You don't want me to complete my college education, I'll drop out today." Although I participated in the Air Force ROTC program and was slated to be commissioned as a second lieutenant, I remember praying, "God, if You don't want me to go into the Air Force, I won't do it."

After this period of evaluation, God did require that I discontinue several activities and plans, including my plan of enlisting in the Air Force. I readily abandoned them. For the first time in my life, I understood by experience what Paul meant when he wrote:

> But whatever was to my profit I now consider loss for the sake of Christ. What is more, I consider everything a loss compared to the surpassing greatness of knowing Christ Jesus my Lord, for whose sake I have lost all things. I consider them rubbish, that I may gain Christ and be found in him, not having a righteousness of my own that comes from the law, but that which is through faith in Christ—the righteousness that comes from God and is by faith. I want to know Christ and the power of his resurrection and the fellowship of sharing in his sufferings, becoming like him in his death.
>
> Philippians 3:7–10

Paul is talking like a man in love—exactly how I felt. Giving my heart and life to Christ was the wisest choice I ever made, and now I was reaping the rewards. I was unconcerned about losing out on earthly pleasures because I had found my reason for existence. My purpose was to be connected to God through Jesus Christ with unparalleled, unimaginable, yet undeserved love. I now wanted to live a purposefully passionate, persistent pursuit of God. I had found *Life*, and I did not want to lose it for anything.

Those first few years of my new life in Christ were filled with zeal. I told everybody about Jesus, whether they wanted to hear about Him or not. For instance, during one math class our instructor was late. Everyone was just idly sitting there, so I got up and began to preach. Twenty minutes later I sat down, and the teacher arrived and started class. This type of behavior was a regular occurrence.

All I wanted to do each day was stay in the presence of the Lord and attend the church I recently had joined. I prayed for hours and hours every day; I disciplined myself to read the Bible; I witnessed to everyone I could. When I did not witness, I felt guilty. If I felt the Lord wanted me to go on a hunger fast and I did not obey, I would cry in disappointment for hours, maybe days, because I wanted to please Him. Any miniscule mistake would bring tears to my eyes. I so over-whelmingly wanted to please God that every ounce of my human strength was spent doing just that.

In two years, however, I reached a point where wisdom taught me a lesson I will never forget. In spite of my ferocious zeal, I reached a point where I had definitely lost something. I hate to admit this, but for the first time, I became miser-able in my Christian experience. Suddenly, I had hit a brick wall. I became so emotionally drained that I did not want to witness anymore. I was deeply discouraged. I was not doing anything wrong; I was not sinning all the time, and I faced no great trial or financial crisis—yet I felt beaten.

What had happened? How had I fallen so far from the peak of joyful bliss in Jesus? The truth is that I had left my "first love," Christ, and had become what I refer to as a "profes-sional" Christian. I was good at attending church, great at leading prayer and excellent in conducting my weekly Bible study. I was a trustworthy and dependable church worker, a great assistant to my pastor. But I had begun to substitute Christian activity for loving God with my whole heart (including my emotions). Christian work replaced Christ as my priority. I had started praying to get answers, while abandoning prayer as a time of fellowship with God. I had begun reading the Bible as a duty and not as a delightful time of drawing nearer to the Lord. I witnessed to others out of obligation rather than out of love for Him. My service in the church was motivated by responsibility rather than relationship. A couple years of this led to dryness in my soul and staleness in my spirit. It resulted in discouragement and a loss of strength.

Wisdom revealed to me how I had neglected to focus on the "first and greatest commandment" and how I had begun to concentrate only on good works and Christian activity. I had left the one thing that always continues to reproduce life and joy—a close, personal, ongoing relationship with Jesus Christ. Like the children of Israel, I had unintentionally forsaken the "spring of living water" and dug my own cisterns, so to speak, "broken cisterns that cannot hold water" (Jeremiah 2:13). I had fallen into an age-old trap—a trap as old as Adam and Eve in the Garden of Eden and as old as the Corinthian church. Paul told the saints in Corinth, "But I am afraid that just as Eve was deceived by the serpent's cunning, your minds may somehow be led astray from your sincere and pure devotion to Christ" (2 Corinthians 11:3).

Contrary to wisdom's whisper, I had allowed myself to be wooed away from intense devotion to Jesus Christ. Unfortunately, I often hear reports similar to mine. Hearts and minds of even the most devout Christians seem to struggle with maintaining a passion for God. As Judson Cornwall said, "Worship is always a now activity."[1] In other words, we cannot rely on past revelation or the hope of future inspiration to be passionate today.

This experience taught me a very valuable lesson—one I never plan to forget. I now know my portion. My portion is passion for Jesus. Wisdom has helped me see that my primary pursuit must be what Jesus told us is the first and greatest commandment—love for God. I am called to the fellowship of Jesus Christ, not just to His service. I have learned that service without love often results in a rebuke. This is certainly what happened to the church of Ephesus in Revelation 2:1–7. The Lord told them, "Yet I hold this against you: You have forsaken your first love" (verse 4). There is no grace greater than the power of loving God. It is the center from which all other graces must flow.

Discovering how loving God can change our lives should motivate us to focus on worshiping Him with our entire soul. If we want to live a life where wisdom flows to us, we must become best friends with wisdom's Source. This may be obvious, yet why do most of us find that our zeal wanes? Is keeping up a "working relationship" good enough? Is an appreciation for God's benefit package the best there is? We may need to be reminded daily about why we are Christians in the first place. Here's a little story that will do just that.

What a King!

Years ago, I heard a story about the king of a small village who consistently taught his subjects about justice. He schooled them never to give mercy when justice was due. The king was strict, ensuring swift and proper justice for every wrong committed in his little kingdom. Needless to say, most of his people lived a clean life, fearing the wrath of the king.

There came a day that shook the kingdom. To everyone's amazement, gold was found missing from the king's treasury. Word shot through the monarchy like a bullet. Who would do such a thing? It was unthinkable to steal from other citizens—who would dare rob the king himself? The king decreed that the thief would instantly receive ten public lashes with the whip. No culprit was found, however, and to make matters worse, gold kept disappearing. The thief continued to steal without getting caught, so the king increased the punishment to twenty lashes. The loyal subjects still could not find the culprit. Finally, the king set the punishment for the clever thief at forty lashes. This amounted to the death penalty; no one could survive forty lashes.

After an intense investigation, the criminal finally was found. The people were shocked—the thief was the king's eighty-year-old grandmother! What a dilemma! What would the king do? He had always taught that mercy should never replace justice. Would he pronounce judgment on his grandmother, whom he dearly loved? After all, he had issued the death sentence before he knew the criminal's identity. Would he now be partial and offer her mercy?

The entire village came out on the day of sentencing. A hush was in the air as everyone awaited the king's instructions. He sat on his throne and commanded that the subject be brought forth. When his grandmother was brought out in chains, the crowd gasped in unbelief. A wave of mixed sentiment erupted. Some wanted her freed; others wanted her punished. All were moved deeply.

The king spoke: "Tie the prisoner to the whipping post and expose her back." He then motioned for the executioner to take his post and prepare to exercise his civic responsibility. The king raised his hand slowly in the air, as he had done so many other times to signal the executioner. This time the king hesitated—his grandmother's life was at stake. He stopped the proceedings, got off his throne, took off his robe, untied his grandmother and commanded his subjects to tie him to the pole. He planned to receive the punishment on her behalf. Justice could be served at the same time that mercy was granted.

This touching story reminds us of another King who took off His robe, left His throne and was tied to a tree to receive punishment for the guilty. Humanity had sinned; we were hopelessly guilty before God. His justice demanded a punishment because "the wages of sin is death" (Romans 6:23). But in His love, He wanted to grant mercy so we might go free. King Jesus satisfied justice and mercy at the same time on the cross.

Like Paul, I exclaim in response, "Oh, the depth of the riches of the wisdom and knowledge of God! How unsearchable his judgments, and his paths beyond tracing out!" (Romans 11:33). One reason we lose our zeal for God is because we lose sight of the terrible price our King paid for each of us. Wisdom calls us to not only remember the sacrifice, but to consider the love given to us.

Wisdom will always encourage us to give ourselves for a higher cause. The highest cause wisdom presses us toward is to love God with our whole being. This is exactly what Jesus expressed in what I call Jesus' "wisdom chapter," Matthew 22. It records the day Jesus was tested by His enemies, who asked Him three specific questions. The first was about paying tribute to Caesar. I shared in chapter 3 how Jesus conquered that question with such wisdom that the Pharisees who posed it were left speechless (see verses 15–22).

Two more questions came His way, though, that were designed to trap Him. The second test question came from some Sadducees asking about the resurrection. Jesus silenced

113

His interrogators and astonished the crowd with His answer about how God is God of the living, not of the dead (see verses 23–33).

Jesus was now two for two, and His wisdom-filled response to the third test question may be His greatest answer ever. The Pharisees again got together to challenge Him, and one of them, an expert in the law, asked, "Teacher, which is the greatest commandment in the Law?" (verse 36).

Another way to frame the question would be, "How then should we live?" or "What should we give attention to in our lives?" If Jesus had singled out any one of the Ten Commandments, it would have been a cause for contention. For example, if Jesus had said the greatest commandment was "Thou shall not murder," those who felt that "Thou shalt not commit adultery" was greatest would have challenged Him. But Jesus answered with truth and wisdom: " 'Love the Lord your God with all your heart and with all your soul and with all your mind.' This is the first and greatest commandment" (verses 37–38).

As we explore the beauty of wisdom's admonition to love God with every aspect of our nature, we will see why it is the greatest commandment. When we put God first, not only do other things fall into place, not only are they given to us as well (see Matthew 6:33), but we will also see an incredible flow of wisdom penetrating our minds and hearts.

Wisdom Knows Love Satisfies

Wisdom knows love satisfies our souls. Everyone searching for satisfaction seems to know where we can find it. Most think true soul satisfaction can be found in material possessions or a well-paid career. But wisdom is aware that earthly pleasures can never truly satisfy us because we were not made to be satisfied with stuff. We were made with a strong desire for pleasure, but the fulfillment of that desire is in God. Consider Psalm 16:11: "You have made known to me the path of life; you will fill me with joy in your presence, with eternal pleasures at your right hand." Wisdom knows true pleasure can only be found in His presence, and the path of life leads only to His right hand.

My all-time favorite television commercial is the classic Wendy's ad where three elderly ladies are sitting at a counter with a huge hamburger bun about eight inches in diameter. They are admiring the bun, but there is no meat in sight. One lady says, "It certainly is a big bun."

Another woman answers, "It's a very big bun."

The first then says, "A big, fluffy bun."

Her friend replies, "It's a very big, fluffy bun."

At that moment, the first lady lifts the top bun and exposes a small piece of beef about three inches in diameter resting on the bottom bun. They scrutinize this small piece of meat, and the third lady forcefully asks, "Where's the beef?"

The announcer then promotes Wendy's hamburgers, and at the end, the little lady forcefully asks one more time, "Where's the beef?"

I often think of this commercial when considering wisdom. For most people, the most satisfying part of a sandwich is the meat, not the bread. We do not need to go through life eating the equivalent of a meatless sandwich. We must find life's fulfilling substance. We must discover what is real and abiding. True wisdom consistently searches for that which surpasses. It will not rest until it leads and links you with what is better, and then with what is best. It is inquisitive by nature—always asking how, what and why. It leads you to ask many questions, and when these are answered, it immerses you in its fruit.

Solomon, the wisest man who ever lived, certainly searched for wisdom's answers. The book of Ecclesiastes is a summary of his search for the meaning of life. He said, "I devoted myself to study and to explore by wisdom all that is done under heaven" (Ecclesiastes 1:13).

Have you ever pondered the purpose or meaning of life? Have you ever contemplated what you need to do to get the most out of life? I certainly have. Through wisdom, Solomon sought the true meaning of life on earth. He was looking for what is valid, what satisfies and fulfills. Consider how deeply and diligently he sought answers:

I thought in my heart, "Come now, I will test you with pleasure to find out what is good." But that also proved to be meaningless. "Laughter," I said, "is foolish. And what does pleasure accomplish?" I tried cheering myself with wine, and embracing folly—my mind still guiding me with wisdom. I wanted to see what was worthwhile for men to do under heaven during the few days of their lives.

I undertook great projects: I built houses for myself and planted vineyards. I made gardens and parks and planted all kinds of fruit trees in them. I made reservoirs to water groves of flourishing trees. I bought male and female slaves and had other slaves who were born in my house. I also owned more herds and flocks than anyone in Jerusalem before me. I amassed silver and gold for myself, and the treasure of kings and provinces. I acquired men and women singers, and a harem as well—the delights of the heart of man. I became greater by far than anyone in Jerusalem before me. In all this my wisdom stayed with me.

I denied myself nothing my eyes desired;
    I refused my heart no pleasure.
My heart took delight in all my work,
    and this was the reward for all my labor.

Ecclesiastes 2:1–10

This is quite a confession! Look at all Solomon accomplished during his search. What a list—there was almost nothing Solomon did not try. First, he joined the "if it feels good, do it" club. He literally tested his heart with pleasure to see if the answer to the meaning of life was in enjoying yourself to the max, but he did not find it there. Then Solomon thought that perhaps it was in laughter, but the Jeff Foxworthy and Bill Cosby of his day could not help him. He then took the substance abuse route; he went for wine and foolishness. That did not work either. Consistently visiting happy hour still left him sad. Solomon then tried to take the business mogul route. He went after houses and vineyards, gardens, parks and ponds. Perhaps he thought since pleasure, laughter and wine did not do it, maybe he needed more stuff. Solomon even had male and female slaves and flocks of animals larger than any other person in Jerusalem. Talk about stuff! Solomon was loaded!

Along with the previously mentioned items, Solomon amassed a huge treasure chest of liquid assets. When he said that he amassed silver and gold and the treasure of kings and provinces, he really meant it. Look at his yearly paycheck: "The weight of the gold that Solomon received yearly was 666 talents" (1 Kings 10:14). That is almost 25 tons—50,000 pounds—$1.33 billion in today's money! Nor does this take into account what Solomon required in his trading with the Arabian kings. If money could make you happy and help you buy life, Solomon would have known it.

Gratefulness is a unique aspect of wisdom that goes with fulfillment. Understanding that what you have comes from the Source of all things creates a desire not just to receive from Him, but to know Him for His sake. Possessing the stuff does not make us grateful. It is knowing the Source of the stuff that allows us to see that we have enough, especially if we really know God as a loving and giving Father. Gratefulness allows wisdom to transfer our struggling with what we do not have into accepting the will of a Father who definitely knows best. Let's become grateful!

Prayer of Gratefulness for Provision

Heavenly Father, I thank You for the provisions and blessings You have given me and my family. I confess that at times I have not been as grateful as I should be. I repent for not recognizing that You have truly blessed me with wealth. Please forgive me. I acknowledge that You are the Giver of all good gifts. I desire to be content with the blessings You have given to me. I ask You to help me thank You for the things that I have, and not dwell on the things I don't have. I know worldly stuff will never fulfill me as only You can. I know true fulfillment can only come from being in Your presence. I believe You are hearing and answering my prayer. Thank You for helping me find what truly satisfies and fulfills. In Jesus' name I pray, Amen.

Our nature is the reason things can never satisfy us. We are made of three distinct parts: body, soul and spirit (see 1 Thessalonians 5:23). Through our body we have world-consciousness, through our soul we have self-consciousness and through our spirit we have God-consciousness. Our body is satisfied with food, clothing and shelter. Our soul is thriving when we feel love, acceptance, belonging and self-esteem. But our spirit—what can fulfill the human spirit? Our human spirit was created to be in constant fellowship with God, who is Spirit. That is why we can have everything we need for our outward person, while our inward person may be empty. You probably have heard it said that there is a God-shaped vacuum in each of us that only God can fill. Ultimate satisfaction is impossible without divine action. The more we learn by wisdom's prompting to love God with all our heart, mind, soul and strength, the more we will be settled and satisfied. Wisdom cannot fully develop in us unless we actively respond to this prompt. Let's decree that we will respond.

Decree That Wisdom Will Cultivate Love

Father, I decree and declare that wisdom will lead me into a deeper love relationship with You. I declare that I will fervently love You with all I am. Let there be a fence of wisdom surrounding me, allowing me to cultivate a beautiful garden of intimacy with You. I declare that I will relentlessly pursue You and Your divine presence. Father, I believe these decrees agree with Your Word, and I sow them into the atmosphere as a measure of faith. In Jesus' name I declare these things, Amen.

Love-Motivated Service

Wisdom knows that service is motivated by love. Not only is love satisfying, but it is also a superior motive for our service to God. The biblical account of Jacob and his two wives, Leah and Rachel, helps us understand why wisdom leads us to pursue love. After deceiving his brother, Esau, Jacob ran away from the family home to live with his uncle Laban. This uncle had two unmarried daughters. Scripture tells us, "Leah had weak eyes, but Rachel was lovely in form, and beautiful" (Genesis 29:17). Laban asked Jacob what he wanted as pay for his service. Jacob answered, "I'll work for you seven years in return for your younger daughter Rachel" (verse 18). Laban agreed.

Serving seven years for a wife was amazing enough, but more amazing was the testimony of Jacob's experience during those seven years. "So Jacob served seven years to get Rachel, but they seemed like only a few days to him because of his love for her" (verse 20). Imagine—7 years, or 365 weeks or 2,555 days felt like just a few days. Jacob must have really loved her! Seven years is long enough for anyone to change his mind along the way, become tired or just give up, yet Jacob did not.

The irony does not stop there. Laban deceived Jacob and gave him Leah instead of Rachel. He awoke to kiss his new bride and realized he had been hoodwinked. Jacob confronted his uncle, who said, "It is not our custom here to give the younger daughter in marriage before the older one. Finish this daughter's bridal week; then we will give you the younger one also, in return for another seven years of work" (verses 26–27).

Jacob agreed and served yet another seven years—fourteen years of service total for his heart's desire. Every woman reading this is probably saying, "Oh, how wonderful!" Most male readers are countering, "Man, she had him wrapped around her finger!"

Whichever way you view the course of events, look at the power of love. Love was an unrelenting motivator churning within Jacob, causing his duty to be delightful. It became Bengay to his sore muscles, Gatorade to his thirst and protein bars to his tired body. It pushed him past the limits of his natural zeal and reason. It was a persistent drive to connect with the object of his affection. It was so powerful that the thought of one day being with Rachel was enough to keep him going. It was not something he acted out; it was something that acted on him. It was a fierce but friendly force to which he willingly yielded. It was power, irresistible power—love's power. No wonder wisdom promotes love to such a degree.

Each of us is called to serve the Lord and obey His commandments. But wisdom suggests a superior motive for our service. We could serve out of a sense of duty, almost feeling as though we have to or else. But this motivation is not very fun, and people serving in such a manner usually burn out easily. We could also serve from fear, being afraid of what God might do if we do not serve. Serving in this manner usually causes a person to do just enough to get by. Or we could choose wisdom's choice and serve out of an overflow of love. This sounds much better. It should, because heaven's wisdom is always right!

What if we loved God half as much as Jacob loved Rachel? Jesus can do far more for us than Rachel ever did for Jacob. Rachel affected Jacob temporally—Jesus affects us eternally. She may have ministered to Jacob's body and soul, but Jesus ministers to us body, soul and spirit. She may have been beautiful, but our Bridegroom is "altogether lovely" (Song of Songs 5:16). He is worthy of our passion and deserving of our affection. Oh, that we might be awestruck by His awesomeness and bewildered by His beauty, captivated by His countenance and conquered by His character!

Extravagant Giving

Wisdom knows that love produces extravagant giving. Matthew provides an extraordinary example of how passion leads to extravagance. A few days before His death, Jesus was eating in the house of Simon the leper. Mary of Bethany entered with a very costly alabaster box full of precious perfume. She broke the box and poured the perfume on Jesus, wiping His feet with her hair. When she did, the room was filled with the smell. The disciples were filled with indignation. They responded to her action with a challenge: "Why this waste?" they asked. "This perfume could have been sold at a high price and the money given to the poor" (Matthew 26:8–9).

Here is my question: Can anything you lavish on God really be a waste? The cost of Mary's perfume, 300 pence, was about $25,000. To understand this deed, I first have to wrap my mind around a bottle of perfume that is so costly. I then have to imagine breaking the whole bottle intentionally and wiping it on the head and the hair of a man who will die in a few days. Yet Mary knew this was no ordinary man; this was Christ Jesus, who is still worthy of our most expensive and excessive sacrifice.

Such an expensive bottle definitely represented Mary's past, present and future. What made her so willing to lavish her life on Christ? It was the power of love. When love touches your heart, you can give everything away and it means nothing to you. Solomon wrote about love's power when he penned, "Many waters cannot quench love; rivers cannot wash it away. If one were to give all the wealth of his house for love, it would be utterly scorned" (Song of Songs 8:7).

A true measure of love has always been the willingness to give to the one you love. Jesus puts it this way: "Where your treasure is, there your heart will be also" (Matthew 6:21). A person's heart always follows his or her treasure. When God is your treasure, your earthly treasures follow that love and giving is automatic. If your earthly treasure is what you prize the most, giving becomes difficult and hoarding will be the result. This is why wisdom's fruit and leading is toward love. Love produces more Christlike character in us.

He First Loved Me

One of the main ways to grow in love toward God is to meditate on how much He loves us. "We love because he first loved us" (1 John 4:19). When we get a revelation of how much He loves us, it radically alters our love quotient. I fully agree with Brennan Manning, author of *The Furious Longing of God*, who wrote,

> If you took the love of all the best mothers and fathers who ever lived (think about that for a moment)—all the goodness, kindness, patience, fidelity, wisdom, tenderness, strength and love—and united all those virtues in one person, that person would only be a faint shadow of the love and mercy in the heart of God for you and me.[2]

A few years ago I experienced God's love in an unusual way. I had been praying for several weeks, asking God to show me how much He loved me. I did not feel needy; I just wanted to experience His love to a greater extent. One day I was sitting on the floor playing with my two young sons, Paul and Chris. Suddenly, I was struck with unbelievable love for them—I was beside myself. There was such a strong bond that I cannot describe it in words. I felt this love until it was almost painful. I sat there and looked at those boys and just wept—not from sadness—I was touched by the power of God. At that moment I felt the Lord Jesus communicating this to my heart: "You love them, don't you?"

I responded in the midst of broken words and tears, "Oh yes, Lord, yes!"

The Lord communicated strongly but compassionately, saying, "Infinitely more than what you feel for them is how I feel for you."

I was ruined. My heart was touched deeply, and my love for God soared to new heights.

You, too, can comprehend more of God's love for you. You may not have an unusual experience, as I did, but as you meditate on the Scriptures that speak of God's love, He can reveal Himself to you in an unprecedented way. As you receive His love, your love for Him will soar.

Wisdom's greatest commandment to love God with all we have has great benefits for us. We will look in the next chapter at the second-greatest commandment, to love our neighbors as ourselves. But first, let's explore our love for God with the tools below.

QUESTIONS FOR MEDITATION

1. Evaluate your love for God by creating a time line from the point of your birth until now. Mark high points and low points in your relationship. Did your level of giving or service indicate some of these peaks and valleys? What helped stimulate the high points? How could this knowledge help you press forward in loving God? Try to identify whatever contributed to the low points in your relationship. What things might you avoid or be aware of in order to avoid these valleys?

2. What have you been inspired to do that goes beyond your normal range of strength, education or experience? Where did the inspiration come from? How did it create motivation within you? Did you feel fulfilled after you did it? What did you accomplish? Did you feel that God inspired you to go to such lengths?

PRACTICAL TIPS

1. Consider a time when you felt overwhelming love for someone. Perhaps it was when a baby was born and you first saw the little face of someone so new. Or perhaps it was when someone you loved was hurt and your concern for their well-being ignited recognition in you of the extent of your love. Take a few moments to relive

that moment. Ask God to speak His love to your heart in an overwhelming way so you can allow your love for Him to soar.

2. Make time in your monthly schedule for a mini-retreat. The goal is to grow in your relationship with God. Create an atmosphere of total focus on Him. You may need to visit a location that inspires you. Leave electronic devices and other distracting items in a different location. Press in, evaluate, listen, create, talk . . . and love Him!

7

Wisdom's Second Commandment

> " 'Love the Lord your God with all your heart
> and with all your soul and with all your mind.'
> This is the first and greatest commandment.
> And the second is like it: 'Love your neighbor
> as yourself.' All the Law and the Prophets
> hang on these two commandments."
>
> —Matthew 22:37–40

I lived in New York City from my birth to my early teens. Our neighborhood in the Lower East Side was multiethnic and a decent place to live. Down the street, however, was a housing project where many gang members lived—mostly Puerto Ricans. We frequently saw these "bad guys" since the path to the closest store ran directly through our plaza. Several times during my childhood, these gang members robbed me. They would wait for me to come out of the store, then they would take whatever change I had, my book bag or my bus pass. I grew weary of the assaults, but I did not know what to do. I could not stay locked in the house all the time.

As I grew older, my parents thought I had learned how to handle the situation. Since there had been no recent major incidents, they decided to fulfill my dream—a shiny red bicycle I had my eye on for years. When they presented it to me for Christmas, I was beside myself. It was a deep, candy-apple red with shiny new reflectors.

A couple days after I received it, I went for a ride. Nine gang members blocked my way. The leader demanded that I give him the bike. Afraid but determined, I refused. I gripped the handlebars tightly and clutched my legs around the bike as hard as possible. Several gang members grabbed me, threw me off the bike and began to beat me. Two of them took off on my bike. The beating hurt, but not half as much as seeing my red bike disappearing around the corner with strangers on it.

I was devastated. Once the gang finished beating me, I ran home in a pile of tears and bruises to tell my dad. I will never forget the pain I saw in his face. He went to the closet to retrieve a hammer and said, "Let's go." We walked directly to the housing project, looking for my bike and a good fight. Thankfully, we never found either. I sometimes think about what might have happened if we had.

That day negatively impacted me—my heart turned against Puerto Ricans. Whenever I saw a Hispanic, whether male or female, young or old, I felt a bit of anger and disdain. I was wounded, and I took it out on anyone who looked or spoke like the ones who had hurt me.

As I grew up, my heart did not change. I did not hate Puerto Ricans, but I certainly did not like them much, either. The Bible says to love your neighbor as yourself, but I would never mug myself or steal a bike from me. How was I to love them like that? I wrestled with this commandment for a while, especially after I committed my life to Jesus. But the commandment remained in spite of my feelings.

A bit later, I will tell you how this story ends. For now, we must realize that we cannot shrink commandments to our level of experience. They are truth to our lives and must be followed at all cost. True wisdom would never lead us down a dead-end street. When Jesus spoke by wisdom and gave us the second-greatest commandment, He knew exactly what He was doing. He knew it would be best for humanity. Let's explore a few examples of extraordinary love and forgiveness for one's neighbors. Then we will examine a few practical ways that we can show love to our neighbors and enemies alike. How about riding off into this adventure with me on our imaginary new red bike?

Impossible Love?

I sometimes wish wisdom's admonition stopped at the greatest commandment, without adding the second. It seems much easier to love God with all of our heart than to love our neighbor. God is perfect; humans are flawed. The Lord is consistent; humans are not. We are promised a reward for what we do for God, but what we do for others often goes unnoticed and unrewarded. Nonetheless, wisdom requires us to love the seemingly unlovable.

As I already mentioned, wisdom requires self-sacrifice. It will never lead us to live only for self, but will drive us to serve others. Wisdom is not just about receiving answers to challenges. It has a nature and character attached to it. Wisdom that comes from sacrificing our own desires will lead us to live in the same manner Jesus lived and to love our neighbor in practical ways.

Many people struggle with the responsibility we have to serve humanity. In fact, many of us even attempt to rationalize loving others away, as did the lawyer who approached Jesus one day. An expert in the law, he asked Jesus which neighbors he must love—an effort on his part to justify treating some people in an ungodly manner. Jesus used the parable of the good Samaritan to illustrate both whom we should love and how we should love them (see Luke 10:30–37). He told about how a priest and Levite both passed by a man who was lying robbed and beaten, while only a Samaritan took the time to stop and care for him. Then Jesus asked the lawyer, "Which of these three do you think was a neighbor to the man who fell into the hands of robbers?" Of course, the lawyer correctly answered that it was the man who had taken pity on him. "Go and do likewise," Jesus instructed him (verses 36–37).

This parable is significant because the Samaritans and Jews had been bitter enemies for decades. The bitterness was so entrenched that a Jewish person would have absolutely nothing to do with Samaritans, who were considered ceremonially unclean, as well as socially impure. The wounded Jew was cared for by someone he probably despised. This parable is potent because the Samaritan likewise would have viewed the Jewish person as an enemy, a stranger and a foreigner. Yet nothing in the natural comes close to the kindness this Samaritan showed. Additionally, were the roles reversed, there is some question as to whether the religious Jew would have shown the same kindness to the Samaritan.

The neighbor we must love is not just our friend, family member, co-worker or acquaintance. It is the beggar on the street, as well as the banker who may have said no when we applied for a loan. This parable illustrates how love is anything but convenient. Why did the priest and Levite pass on by when they saw this wounded man? Perhaps they had important Temple affairs to attend to, or maybe they were late for the Saturday Sabbath service. But loving your neighbor often means delaying your plans for the benefit of someone else.

Loving your neighbor can also mean putting your life in danger. It is possible that the priest and Levite failed to stop because the steep and winding road to Jericho was unsafe, with many places for thieves to hide. Perhaps they thought the man was a decoy and that stopping to help would draw thieves out of hiding to attack.

Loving your neighbor will also cost you resources. The Samaritan spent his own money to care for this ailing man. True neighbors who truly love will risk much for the welfare of another person. This is what wisdom commands.

Prayer to Love Our Neighbors

Lord Jesus, help me to see the needs around me with Your eyes. Grant me Your grace so that I will be an extension of Your kindness and love. Help me obey wisdom's admonition to love my neighbor as myself. Make me sensitive to the hurts of others. I ask this in Jesus' name, Amen.

Radical Wisdom: Love Your Enemies

As if loving your neighbor were not hard enough, now Jesus ups the ante. As simple as loving another person sounds, many struggle with it. For example, reexamine the parable Jesus told about the man on the road to Jericho. Many would reason that the man was too careless. Did he not know it was a dangerous road? Why did he not have bodyguards? Why should I use my money and time to nurse him back to health? He only got what he deserved, right? My helping would enable his carelessness next time!

Most of us realize there are those less fortunate than ourselves who need a helping hand, so we give to mission agencies. However, helping the needy by activating the love of Jesus can be quite costly. It forces us to put aside our criteria and stop judging others, even if we feel justified in doing so. It takes "dying to self" to make a difference to someone who we feel does not deserve our help. Does this sound like wisdom to your natural self?

In loving others, we must put aside our own preferences and modes of operation, submitting them to a higher wisdom. This alone can be hard to swallow, yet Jesus pushes the envelope further with His next command:

"You have heard that it was said, 'Love your neighbor and hate your enemy.' But I tell you: Love your enemies and pray for those who persecute you, that you may be sons of your Father in heaven. He causes his sun to rise on the evil and the good, and sends rain on the righteous and the unrighteous. If you love those who love you, what reward will you get? Are not even the tax collectors doing that? And if you greet only your brothers, what are you doing more than others? Do not even pagans do that? Be perfect, therefore, as your heavenly Father is perfect."

Matthew 5:43–48

What kind of wisdom is this? This radical statement necessitates a definition for such a basic word as *love*. The Greek language has three words for love. The word *eros* is romantic love. A second word, *philia*, is friendship love, love that is reciprocated. The third word is *agape*. This love seeks nothing in return. This is the kind of love God has, and He desires that it operate easily in our hearts. When *agape* is present, it makes no difference whether we like a person or not; we simply love him or her because God does. Agape causes us to love a person who does evil, although we may hate the evil he or she did. This is such a superior way of living, it is no wonder wisdom advocates this lifestyle.

Martin Luther King Jr. impacted the world with his philosophy of nonviolent love. He grew up in segregated times, when life was miserable for most blacks—especially in the South. In King's book *Strength to Love*, he had this to say about loving your enemies:

> With every ounce of our energy we must continue to rid this nation of the incubus of segregation. But we shall not in the process relinquish our privilege and our obligation to love. While abhorring segregation, we shall love the segregationist. This is the only way to create the beloved community.
>
> To our most bitter opponents we say: "We shall match your capacity to inflict suffering by our capacity to endure suffering. We shall meet your physical force with soul force. Do to us what you will, and we shall continue to love you. We cannot in all good conscience obey your unjust laws, because noncooperation with evil is as much a moral obligation as is cooperation with good. Throw us in jail, and we shall still love you. Send your hooded perpetrators of violence into our community at the midnight hour and beat us and leave us half dead, and we shall still love you. But be ye assured that we will wear you down by our capacity to suffer. One day we shall win freedom, but not only for ourselves. We shall so appeal to your heart and your conscience that we shall win you in the process, and our victory would be a double victory."[1]

Martin Luther King's house was bombed and he received every death threat imaginable, yet he could speak in this manner. What could possibly be our excuse? Actually, Dr. King did not just speak love, he lived it—consistently fighting evil with good—or I should say with wisdom!

As usual, wisdom is superior in its admonition. History has proven over and over that one of the reasons we should love our enemies is because love is the only force suitable for transforming an enemy into a comrade. It is impossible to win opponents who hate us with hate. Hate is revengeful and destructive. It seeks no goodwill for its neighbor—only getting even. Love, on the other hand, has the power to build up and redeem. It will restore and revive. Naturally, love does not negate the need for justice and judgment. On the contrary, it invites it. But when carried out with a motive of love, justice and judgment become pure and impartial.

Prayer to Love Our Enemies

Heavenly Father, thank You in advance for giving me the ability to love my enemies not just in theory or in word, but also in truth. Let the manifestation of Your second-greatest commandment be an agape love through me that seeks nothing in return. I realize the key to this is to forgive people. Help me forgive others quickly, just as You have forgiven me. I now choose to forgive all those who have wronged or hurt me. Thank You for Your grace that will enable me to love them in the way You command. In Jesus' name, Amen.

Wisdom Lays Down Its Life

Twelve million people live in Calcutta, India. New York City has 11,500 people per square mile, but Calcutta has 57,000 people per square mile. It is one of the most crowded cities in the world. Almost half the people in Calcutta live in slums. The smell of trash and debris is sometimes smothering. Many of these people line the roadsides and beg for money.

This is the city in which Mother Teresa chose to serve. She found a woman on the street who was partially eaten by rats and whom the hospital refused to treat. This incident motivated her to ask for a place to care for those dying in the city. The authorities gave her an abandoned building attached to a tiny Hindu shrine, but the Hindu priests did not want her there. The idea of a Christian woman attaching a House of Mercy to their shrine was definitely unappealing, but the city would not reject her. They thought it was a perfect pairing since the shrine had a crematorium. When people died at the House of Mercy, they could be sent next door for cremation.

The Hindu priests next door to Mother Teresa staged protests and demonstrations. They shouted obscenities and stirred up angry mobs, making death threats against Mother Teresa. Then one of the Kali priests who had been most vocal against her contracted tuberculosis. He continued to get worse and finally collapsed, falling right in front of her door in his own blood and body fluids. A Hindu priest walked right over him because nobody would touch a person in that condition, yet Mother Teresa picked up this man who had been her enemy. She put him on a clean bed, feeding and caring for him until he died. Then she delivered his body to the Hindu temple.

From that point on, protest demonstrations ceased. How could the priests demonstrate against the love of this woman? How could they make death threats when this woman had loved her enemy? Love won over that Hindu shrine. Love will always cause us to win in life. No wonder the second-greatest commandment suggested in Jesus' "wisdom chapter" is to love our neighbor as ourselves.

Wisdom Commands Forgiveness

One inescapable expression of love is to forgive those who wrong us. Jesus taught unequivocally that we must forgive.

His admonition to forgive was so strong that He declared, "For if you forgive men when they sin against you, your heavenly Father will also forgive you. But if you do not forgive men their sins, your Father will not forgive your sins" (Mathew 6:14–15).

God says if we do not forgive others, He will not forgive us. Have you needed forgiveness lately? I certainly have. We all do. God demands we give others the same courtesy He offers us—the ability to be forgiven when wronged. The apostle Peter, seeking to find limits on the forgiveness requirement, asked, "Lord, how often shall my brother sin against me, and I forgive him? Up to seven times?"

Jesus said to him, "I do not say to you, up to seven times, but up to seventy times seven" (Matthew 18:21–22, NKJV).

Jesus was not saying, "Keep a journal and forgive up to 490 times, but on the 491st time you have been offended, you have My permission to take revenge." This is not what He meant. He taught that there is no limit to the number of times you forgive.

As believers, we must guard against the devastating effects of unforgiveness. Like a cancerous tumor, it devours healthy hearts and destroys vital relationships. Human nature and demonic influence cause a natural drift toward this poison. It is not difficult to bear a grudge or harbor unforgiveness. Rather, it can be tough at times to let offenses go. Scripture warns of an epidemic of "cold love" as we near the end of the age. Speaking of the end times, Jesus says, "Because of the increase of wickedness, the love of most will grow cold" (Matthew 24:12). It does not matter if the world around us is insensitive; we must still radiate the agape love of God through forgiving others. This is a battle we cannot afford to lose.

You will have an opportunity to exercise forgiveness multiple times in your life. You will be mistreated before you die.

All of us will have opportunity to sing a verse of the "Somebody Done Somebody Wrong Song." Jesus even said offenses will come—it is not a matter of if, but when. When it happens, wisdom demands we respond in love and forgiveness.

Conquering Enemies with Love

Love is required if wisdom is to fully impact in our lives. Forgiveness is the first step, but God often requires love to continue beyond this step to be sure our hearts are ready to receive His wisdom. Philip Yancey, in his book *Rumors of Another World*, tells the following story of how a person pursued love far beyond forgiveness.

> Nelson Mandela taught the world a lesson in grace when, after emerging from prison after twenty-seven years and being elected president of South Africa, he asked his jailer to join him on the inauguration platform. He then appointed Archbishop Desmond Tutu to head an official government panel with a daunting name, the Truth and Reconciliation Commission. Mandela sought to defuse the natural pattern of revenge that he had seen in so many countries where one oppressed race or tribe took control from another.
>
> For the next two-and-a-half years, South Africans listened to the reports of atrocities coming out of the TRC hearings. The rules were simple: if a white policeman or army officer voluntarily faced his accusers, confessed his crime, and fully acknowledged his guilt, he could not be tried and punished for that crime. Hard-liners grumbled about the obvious injustice of letting criminals go free, but Mandela insisted that the country needed healing even more than it needed justice.
>
> At one hearing, a policeman named van de Broek recounted an incident when he and other officers shot an eighteen-year-old boy and burned the body, turning it on the fire like a piece of barbecue meat in order to destroy the evidence. Eight years

later, van de Broek returned to the same house and seized the boy's father. The wife was forced to watch as policemen bound her husband on a woodpile, poured gasoline over his body, and ignited it.

The courtroom grew hushed as the elderly woman who had lost first her son and then her husband was given a chance to respond. "What do you want from Mr. van de Broek?" the judge asked. She said she wanted van de Broek to go to the place where they had burned her husband's body and gather up the dust so she could give him a decent burial. His head down, the policeman nodded agreement.

Then the woman added a further request: "Mr. van de Broek took all my family away from me, and I still have a lot of love to give. Twice a month, I would like for him to come to the ghetto and spend a day with me so I can be a mother to him. And I would like Mr. van de Broek to know that he is forgiven by God, and that I forgive him too. I would like to embrace him so he can know my forgiveness is real."

Spontaneously, some in the courtroom began singing "Amazing Grace" as the elderly woman made her way to the witness stand, but van de Broek did not hear the hymn. He had fainted, overwhelmed.[2]

Hear the voice of wisdom that calls beyond the hurts you have experienced and the people who may have encamped against you. Discover the joy of forgiveness and the blessing of love. Wisdom's second-greatest commandment to love your neighbor as yourself has profound benefits for both the giver and the receiver.

Prayer for Wisdom to Love

Heavenly Father, I thank You for giving me the wisdom to walk in love. Your Word gives great examples of how *love* is an action word and not a mere feeling. Give me the grace to be like the good Samaritan and not overlook those in need or wax cold toward the seemingly unlovable. Let my response be according to love because love never fails. In Jesus' name, Amen.

Wisdom Gave Me Love

Now I need to take you back to my issue with Hispanics. After I became a Christian, I knew I had to obey this commandment to love my neighbor; there was no choice in the matter. Avoiding people of Hispanic background did not satisfy it. I struggled, but finally I allowed God to help me see things in a different light. After all, I, too, had hurt people. I may never have robbed people or stolen bikes—but there were people I had hurt. I was not perfect; I needed forgiveness. I also realized that the grudge I held against the Hispanics hurt *me* more than anyone else. It kept me from flowing in wisdom's release.

Once I set my heart to forgive and love Hispanic people, it did not take long for my feelings to change. I simply released the offense, refusing to hold on to it mentally or emotionally. Negative thoughts returned at times, but I released them. In a short while, my heart felt more normal when I saw and heard people of Hispanic origin. No negative drag pulled me into thinking ill of them. By God's grace there had been a transformation.

A few months ago I held a conference in my church to honor the Hispanic people in my community. After the conference, my assistant pastor commented on how much the Hispanic people were drawn to me. He said, "Pastor, I don't know much, but one thing I know is that these definitely are your people."

Oh, the power of love—wisdom's love—transforming love!

Jesus called them together and said, "You know that the rulers of the Gentiles lord it over them, and their high officials exercise authority over them. Not so with you. Instead, whoever wants to become great among you must be your servant, and whoever wants to be first must be your slave—just as the Son of Man did not come to be served, but to serve, and to give his life as a ransom for many."

Mathew 20:25–28

I like to remind myself daily that Jesus came to serve, not to be served. If I want to be great, I must think like a servant and a slave. I must serve and give my life for others. It is not easy, but it is wisdom's way.

Wisdom may seem demanding in its command to love. However, we are not done yet! Wisdom will also show us how to purify ourselves on a new level. We will deal with this in the next chapter. First, however, cement this chapter into your life with the questions and tips below.

QUESTIONS FOR MEDITATION

1. Do you know someone who has wronged or hurt you in a way that seems hard to forgive? Is there any incident with any person that returns to your remembrance every now and then? Make sure you release your feelings toward anyone you may hold a grudge against. Be sure to release any hold you have on those feelings, as well. Let wisdom play a new song in your head.

2. Do you struggle with any particular people, race or ethnicity? Do you ever find yourself feeling even a little disdain toward those who are less well off than you? Ask God to reveal any hidden places where you have stored negative feelings or misplaced anger. Ask Him to grace you to receive wisdom's fullness in the form of loving these people.

The famed Sermon on the Mount, taught by Jesus and re-corded in Matthew chapters 5 through 7, lists many practical ways we can show love to our neighbors. Let me summarize a few of its key principles. If we practice these, we will be well on our way to walking in love.

- Refrain from anger toward your brethren.
- Do not speak evil of your brethren.
- Before you offer anything to God, make sure to settle offenses others have against you.
- Settle matters quickly with those who have anything against you.
- Keep your heart pure toward the opposite sex.
- Remain faithful to your spouse.
- Be a person of your word.
- Love your enemies.
- Pray for those who persecute you.
- Give to the needy in an honorable way, not showing off.
- Consider yourself before assessing others' wrongs.

This list is quite all-inclusive, but let me share one practical thing that helps me remember the second-greatest commandment. I keep a stack of index cards with me on which I have written Scriptures and principles that I wish to live out daily. One of those cards has the title "Servant" at the top and some of the Scriptures from the Sermon on the Mount written under it. You could try this as well.

8

Wisdom Comes Clean

Who may ascend the hill of the LORD?
Who may stand in his holy place?
He who has clean hands and a pure heart.

—Psalm 24:3–4

I have a dear friend named Terrance who is pastor of a church in another city in Alabama. He told me about an email he received from a pastor in Ghana. This young minister, Kunta, expressed his need to find a "father in the Gospel." He shared with Terrance how he had never had a spiritual father and was seeking someone to mentor him. He had met up with another pastor who had advised, "If you are looking for a true father, I highly recommend Pastor Terrance." This touched Terrance's heart deeply. In spite of the distance between them, they began getting acquainted via the Internet. Terrance now had a new son in the faith.

This young African became a model son. After preaching in his own church service, he called Terrance every Sunday to give a report of how the Holy Spirit had moved. He testified to dozens of salvations, healings and powerful miracles. Kunta would also bring his problems before Terrance and ask for advice and wise counsel. He was a needy but grateful African minister thrilled to finally have a wise and caring father.

After a few months, Kunta decided to hold a crusade. He elicited Terrance's prayer support as he began to plan the three-day event for fifty thousand people at a local stadium. Terrance appreciated the zeal of this young pastor and affirmed him along the way. He was impressed with Kunta's advertising strategy, his website and his energy toward the crusade.

Terrance was delighted to financially support his new son in ministry. He saw this as an opportunity to sow funds into Africa—an often needy continent. He felt so proud when he received the crusade report stating that several thousand souls came to Christ during the event. It was money well spent.

Kunta and Terrance continued their weekly calls and mentoring relationship. During one call, Kunta pitched the idea of sponsoring a pastors' conference. Since Terrance has a real heart for training pastors, he readily agreed. Kunta insisted that Terrance join them for the conference. He felt it would not be right to train pastors without his pastor/father in attendance. He also needed financial help for the conference, so Terrance sent money to undergird the event and agreed to come. Terrance was excited that he would have the opportunity to impact pastors side by side with his spiritual son.

A few days before Pastor Terrance was to leave for Ghana, he received a dreadful call. Kunta informed him of a devastating tragedy that had just occurred. While his wife and three children were driving home after Sunday service, they were killed in a car accident, burned beyond recognition. Kunta could not be comforted because he felt responsible for the accident. He explained to Terrance how his wife did not want to go home after church that day, but he ignored her, compelling her to take the kids home. Had he not insisted his wife leave, she and the children would still be alive.

Terrance tried to minister to Kunta, but the young man was distraught and overwhelmed with grief. The next call hit Terrance at the core of his being. One of Kunta's church members informed him that Kunta had committed suicide. Feeling he could no longer live without his wife and children, he drank deadly poison. The church's leadership team canceled the pastors' conference and focused on burying the first family. They needed money for the funeral, so Pastor Terrance responded to their needs again. He also talked over the situation with me, and we discussed what could be done for this fledgling church that had lost its leaders. We agreed that it would be best for Terrance to travel to Ghana as soon as possible to help in the transition.

My church has a missions work in Ghana, so I called my Ghanian national coordinator to accompany Terrance once he arrived in the country. The day after Pastor Terrance arrived, my coordinator called to give me an unexpected report. His suspicions had been aroused because news of a pastor and family dying in such a manner would have shot through the church world like a bullet, yet there was no account of these events in the media. He discovered that the names Kunta used were aliases and the conference was feigned. When Terrance persisted in coming to Ghana despite all attempts to dissuade him, they even erected billboards about the conference along the road where Terrance would travel between the airport and the supposed church site. The billboards were up the day he landed and gone the next day.

The setup by these professional thieves was detailed beyond what Terrance could have imagined. They fraudulently created a website using church buildings from one place and different people's pictures from other sites. They altered the photos to look genuine. Kunta and his accomplices disappeared with all the money Pastor Terrance had sent.

These finely crafted lies cost the American pastor tens of thousands of dollars. "Kunta" had devised a master plot that Terrance fell for headlong. Who had wisdom in this situation? Terrance obviously did not. But what about the scam artists? Did Kunta use wisdom to come up with this ploy? Does wisdom have a dark side to it? What is wisdom, anyway? Can it be used for bad purposes?

There are two kinds of wisdom—one to embrace and the other to shun. Motive and fruit distinguish these two polar opposites. I want to show you how to recognize the kind of wisdom God desires that we possess. You will also discover how the origin or source behind your wisdom is vitally important. Let's dissect both forms of wisdom and discover how to discern the form we seek. As we explore the character of true wisdom, we will learn to shun its devious opposite.

True wisdom—godly wisdom—has a certain character. It is important that we learn its character so we do not confuse it with earthly or demonic wisdom. Look what James has to say about the two forms of wisdom:

> Who is wise and understanding among you? Let him show it by his good life, by deeds done in the humility that comes from wisdom. But if you harbor bitter envy and selfish ambition in your hearts, do not boast about it or deny the truth. Such "wisdom" does not come down from heaven but is earthly, unspiritual, of the devil. For where you have envy and selfish ambition, there you find disorder and every evil practice.

> But the wisdom that comes from heaven is first of all pure;
> then peace-loving, considerate, submissive, full of mercy and
> good fruit, impartial and sincere. Peacemakers who sow in
> peace raise a harvest of righteousness.
>
> James 3:13–18

James delineates dual wisdom in the verses above. There is
sensual wisdom originating from a demonic source, and there
is heavenly wisdom whose genesis is the Spirit of God. The
difference in these forms of wisdom is implicit in the character and nature each produces. Wisdom that is from beneath
produces bitterness, jealousy and selfish ambition in the heart.
Some people whom the world calls wise actually possess such
wisdom. Though they may have a degree of wisdom, it is not
the kind that we seek as believers. The origin of wisdom determines its product. Worldly wisdom produces ungodly results,
but spiritual wisdom produces good and desirable results.

The fruit of worldly wisdom is selfish ambition, which
leads to bitterness, jealousy, arrogance, lies and the like. True
wisdom is the polar opposite. It does not urge us to live just
for the moment. True wisdom helps us consider the end of
a thing and how others are affected by what is done. True
wisdom is married to good behavior and deeds.

My introduction to the world of counterfeit wisdom happened when I was a young man in Tuskegee. Scott Johnson
liked my younger sister, Karen. He did everything he could to
impress her. At first Karen was resistant, until Scott dethroned
all her inhibitions by presenting her with a box from a well-
known jewelry store. The ring inside enamored my sister,
and Scott's words were as glowing as the ring. When she saw
the name of the jeweler on the box and what was inside, she
reasoned, *He must truly love me if he spent this much on
me.* As a result, she finally threw herself at him and decided
without reservation that she would be his bride.

Karen's decision was resolute and her commitment was meant to be lifelong—that is, until the gold ring turned green. It started fading within three days and was totally corroded within a week. It was then that we found out Scott had bought the ring from the cheap store downtown and put it in an upscale jewelry box. Though some may consider his act callous or dumb, he considered himself smart or wise. He did not, however, demonstrate true wisdom. It was not wisdom from above because its fruit stunk. Karen was wise to be done with him.

Has God Said?

Satan used worldly wisdom to entice Adam and Eve to eat forbidden fruit. The serpent is described as being "more crafty than any of the wild animals the LORD God had made" (Genesis 3:1). Out of his slyness, the serpent struck up a conversation with Eve, asking,

> "Did God really say, 'You must not eat from any tree in the garden'?"
> The woman said to the serpent, "We may eat fruit from the trees in the garden, but God did say, 'You must not eat fruit from the tree that is in the middle of the garden, and you must not touch it, or you will die.'"
> "You will not surely die," the serpent said to the woman. "For God knows that when you eat of it your eyes will be opened, and you will be like God, knowing good and evil."
>
> Genesis 3:1–5

Do you see what is happening here? Satan does not walk out wearing red pajamas, with horns and a pitchfork, and say, "I want to destroy your life and bring the earth under a curse, so please eat this fruit." He appeals to Eve's desire and reasons with her according to her internal interests. Satan begins to think long and hard, choosing his words, intonation, facial expression and demeanor very carefully. His aim is to deceive Eve using wisdom—but its source is definitely not from heaven.

Interestingly, Satan attempts to trick Eve with the promise of becoming wiser. Genesis 3:6 reports, "When the woman saw that the fruit of the tree was good for food and pleasing to the eye, and also desirable for gaining wisdom, she took some and ate it. She also gave some to her husband, who was with her, and he ate it." Eve yielded to demonic wisdom while seeking godly wisdom, and at the end of the day wound up with a curse. The result was nakedness, shame and suffering that could only be reversed by the coming of the promised Messiah.

Jesus admonished us to be "as shrewd as snakes and as innocent as doves" (Matthew 10:16). Shrewdness is not the problem. The problem is the motive of one's heart. Our motive should always be innocent and helpful, never selfish and hurtful.

I am sure you can think of many other examples of people who manifested sharp mental ability beyond typical knowledge or intelligence, but used it for evil purposes. While this technically might be construed as wisdom, it is not the wisdom we seek. It is hellish wisdom born from beneath and destructive wisdom designed to defile. It is Satan's wisdom, which produces satanic results. Wisdom used for self-aggrandizing purposes is not godly wisdom. We should avoid it at all costs.

Prayer to Expose Earthly, Natural, Demonic Wisdom

Heavenly Father, I thank You in advance for granting me the authority to bind and loose, the authority to cast down and the authority to speak against anything that has not originated from Your throne. Father, expose every earthly, natural or demonic ambition residing in my heart. Increase my discernment to quickly recognize the character of counterfeit wisdom. Destroy the root cause of any earthly wisdom I have. I bind every idea or imagination attempting to enter my mind that is inconsistent with the character of true godly wisdom. I loose the gentleness of true wisdom in my life. Father, I thank You for the victory in Jesus' name, Amen.

Pure Wisdom

Look at another translation of James 3:17: "But the wisdom that is from above is first pure, then peaceable, gentle, willing to yield, full of mercy and good fruits, without partiality and without hypocrisy" (NKJV). In the Greek, the word *first* here is translated from the word *protos*. It signifies first in place, order and time. *Protos* also means first in rank, dignity or meaning. So, let's say that true wisdom is first pure. This would then mean that if wisdom does not have this quality, it is not the true wisdom that comes from God.

The apostle James says that wisdom is pure. Therefore, the quality of wisdom from God is first and foremost pure. Purity means that wisdom is chaste, sanctified and pure from all that is sensual, earthly, demonic and animalistic. If wisdom is pure, then as we receive wisdom from above, its nature will be chaste, holy, sanctified and unmixed.

Several years ago, I was faced with a major problem in the church I pastor. Two ladies—let's call them Lucille and Lawanda—were causing a great deal of trouble, but they were also sneaky. Because they operated behind the scenes, it was difficult to find evidence that could provide me with a teaching moment in which to confront them. Additionally, they possessed such strong personalities that most people would not stand up to them. There was little peace and even less unity in our church because these two catalysts kept stirring up trouble. I did not know what to do, but I knew the situation was delicate. Many people would be negatively affected if I brought correction to these ladies. Our church was small, so any little conflict became larger than life.

The church is in the business of helping people change, yet these ladies would not change. Every attempt failed. I asked God for wisdom in the situation. As I did, a thought popped into my mind: *Pray that they leave the church.* I accepted the thought, taking it as God's wisdom. This seemed similar to what can happen when a person develops a cancerous tumor that threatens the health of the whole body. Sometimes tumors can be shrunk, but at other times they are too invasive—the only solution is to remove them. The second scenario was what was happening with these two ladies.

Three days later, while I was on my knees praying that they would leave peacefully on their own, I received an unforgettable phone call. Both ladies were on the line, but Lucille spoke first. "Pastor," she said, "we have some bad news. We will be leaving the church. This Sunday will be our last. The Lord told me our assignment is complete here and we must move on."

Through smiles they could not see, straining not to let the joy I felt be heard in my voice, I said, "Sisters, you ought to obey what God is telling you. No problem—I understand."

They left the church the following Sunday. A few people were sad, many were glad and the peace of God returned to the church. Due to godly wisdom, a confrontation that could have caused major problems transformed into a smooth self-expulsion.

From that time on, I have noticed that whenever I take time to search for true wisdom's godly solution, the result is

151

usually a pure solution to a volatile problem. But each situation requires wisdom for its unique characteristics. I cannot apply the strategy from the story above to all problem people within my church. There are times that wisdom has prompted me to handle troublesome members in a totally different way. The key is in hearing wisdom's solution.

Prayer for Wisdom from Above

Heavenly Father, I thank You in advance for endowing me with wisdom that flows directly from Your heartbeat. Grace me with wisdom that is first of all pure, then peaceable, gentle, reasonable, filled with Your mercy and bearing good fruit. Father, I want to continually transform into Your image and exude godly wisdom that is unwavering, without hypocrisy. I thank You for being the God who hastens to perform Your Word. Therefore, I now receive Your wisdom from above, by Your grace. In Jesus' name, Amen.

Wisdom's Virtues

Although wisdom is founded first on purity, it also has other equally important characteristics, or virtues. These describe its DNA. When wisdom manifests and we apply it, it produces the fruit of these virtues in our lives, whatever the situation. Besides its purity, wisdom is peaceable, gentle, willing to yield, full of mercy and good fruits, without partiality and without hypocrisy. Let's explore each of these briefly.

Peaceable

Wisdom induces harmony. It has peace, produces peace and functions best in a heart full of peace. Wise individuals labor to preserve peace and to restore peace when it has been broken.

Peace is total well-being and prosperity that manifests as the result of God's presence in our lives. Wisdom will teach you to avoid unnecessary conflict. Some people in your life will choose to become your enemy, but you should never choose to become theirs. Scripture admonishes, "If it is possible, as far as it depends on you, live at peace with everyone" (Romans 12:18).

Wisdom will teach you not to offend unnecessarily. It will instruct you to quickly apologize and make restitution wherever possible. Wisdom realizes the fruitlessness of devaluing valuable relationships. It understands that everyone is made in the image of God and deserves to be treated with dignity and respect. Wisdom does not minimize standards or truth for the sake of peace, but it does choose peace over conflict whenever applicable.

Prayer for Peace

Praise to my Lord, the Prince of Peace. You are the One who calms my spirit when things are raging around me. Help me be still. You spoke and the elements came into existence. With Your authority, I can speak to my spirit and say, "Spirit, be still." I do not want to wrestle with my thoughts. You said in Your Word that we are to seek peace and pursue it. My desire is to find peace and chase after it all my days. When I am at peace, I am at rest. Your Word declares that a heart at peace gives life. My heart depends on You and no other. Thank You for peace and calm in the midst of the storm. In the matchless name of Jesus Christ I pray, Amen.

Gentle

Wisdom is not harsh and dictatorial. It is gentle and forbearing, always making allowances for others. This wisdom is closely tied to the character and nature of Jesus Christ.

153

He said, "Come to me, all you who are weary and burdened, and I will give you rest. Take my yoke upon you and learn from me, for I am gentle and humble in heart, and you will find rest for your souls. For my yoke is easy and my burden is light" (Matthew 11:28–30).

Jesus describes Himself as gentle and lowly of heart. This is the fruit wisdom produces. It does not force or coerce people against their will; it is easygoing. Wisdom shows you there are times when it just is not worth arguing. It also highlights the value of responding to things properly. The more gentle and humble you are in relationships, the more productive they will be. Isaiah described the gentleness of Jesus this way:

> Here is my servant, whom I uphold,
>   my chosen one in whom I delight;
> I will put my Spirit on him
>   and he will bring justice to the nations.
> He will not shout or cry out,
>   or raise his voice in the streets.
> A bruised reed he will not break,
>   and a smoldering wick he will not snuff out.
> In faithfulness he will bring forth justice.
>
> Isaiah 42:1–3

A bruised reed is almost useless, and a dimly burning candlewick does not produce much light. Symbolically speaking, this is telling us that Jesus respects the weakest person and the most bruised individual. He will not add to their plight or pain. The world needs a few more gentlemen and gentlewomen. Wisdom will produce gentleness in you—so pursue wisdom.

Prayer for Gentleness

Father, thank You for the gentleness You have shown me. Lord, I ask that I continually be clothed in gentleness. Grace me with tenderness toward others. I pray that my demeanor would be evidence of Your mercy and compassion toward us. I ask that Your will be done in my life. Show me how to avoid giving in to anger, vengeance, retaliation and bitterness, for these do not produce the life You desire for me. Grace me to be loving, nurturing, comforting and understanding. In Jesus' name, Amen.

Willing to Yield (Easily Entreated)

Wisdom is not hardnosed. It is easily entreated and willing to yield. It is not unreasonable like Abigail's husband, Nabal. At one time, this wealthy man's shepherds were protected by yet-to-be-king David. Although David and his men protected Nabal, there came a time when David's men were needy. While King Saul was chasing David, trying to kill him, David lacked basic food and supplies. He heard that Nabal was celebrating a feast, so he instructed ten of his young men to approach Nabal:

> "Go up to Nabal at Carmel and greet him in my name. Say to him: 'Long life to you! Good health to you and your household! And good health to all that is yours!
>
> " 'Now I hear that it is sheep-shearing time. When your shepherds were with us, we did not mistreat them, and the whole time they were at Carmel nothing of theirs was missing. Ask your own servants and they will tell you. Therefore be favorable toward my young men, since we come at a festive time. Please give your servants and your son David whatever you can find for them.' "
>
> 1 Samuel 25:5–8

I think the request was reasonable. David had protected Nabal's shepherds for several weeks. All he asked for was a little something to eat. However, Nabal responded negatively:

"Who is this David? Who is this son of Jesse? Many servants are breaking away from their masters these days. Why should I take my bread and water, and the meat I have slaughtered for my shearers, and give it to men coming from who knows where?"

1 Samuel 25:10–11

Nabal definitely lacked wisdom. He was neither reasonable nor easily entreated. Because of Nabal's stubbornness, David decided to kill him and all his servants. Then Abigail, Nabal's wife, came and entreated David not to do so, and he relented. David was reasonable and easily entreated, whereas Nabal was not. The incident did cost Nabal his life, however. He dropped dead a few days later, seemingly smitten by God.

How much unnecessary suffering do some people encounter because of their unreasonable, unyielding attitudes? This is not the path of wisdom. It is easy to get along with wisdom and dangerous to try to get along without it.

Decree to Yield to the Lord's Will

Let every rebellious tendency within me be destroyed and uprooted. I decree that the Lord shall have His way in my life. Let God's will be done and not my own. Father, when I lie in my bed at night, search my heart. Into Your hands I commit my spirit and my life. I do not want to be unwilling to yield to Your will. I decree that my desires are Yours. I bind my mind to the mind of Christ, and I say, "Yes, Lord!" I decree change in my mindset and my life; I decree that change has already arrived. I decree that I am a "new me" who does what Christ wants and goes where Christ goes. I decree, "No more rebellion." I declare it is done. I receive it in Jesus' name, Amen.

Full of Mercy

Wisdom is also full of mercy. Mercy is compassion toward the miserable and destitute. Wisdom is not selfish; it thinks about those in misery. Jesus certainly thought about us miserable, lost sinners when He came to earth and submitted to death on the cross. He who *is* wisdom demonstrated it by caring for those who could not care for themselves.

Mercy is demonstrated—not simply felt. The mercy wisdom releases does all it can to assist the less fortunate. It is a fruit of wisdom. You cannot have true wisdom from above and not hurt when others hurt. Wisdom cares!

Full of Good Fruits

Wisdom is profitable. It produces something. It is not lazy or unproductive. It is active and aggressive. No matter what you apply it to, it accomplishes high-level productivity and its fruits are good—not to be discarded or burned. When wisdom produces oranges, they will be good enough to take to market and sell. When wisdom raises children, the outcome will be good (perhaps not perfect . . . but good).

Jesus spoke of the harvest being thirty, sixty or a hundred-fold. Wisdom guarantees the best harvest. If you guide your marriage by wisdom, its fruit will be good. The same goes for your business, your hobbies or your future goals. True wisdom can only produce what is good—nothing rotten and nothing unproductive.

Decree for a Harvest

Lord, You are the real Vine. I decree that nourishment will flow from my new roots as I am grafted into You and as I latch on to Your spirit. I decree that I am rooted in Christ. I decree that all things that need to be harvested, born and

157

manifested in my life are done now in the name of Jesus. Everything that began as a seed must be born, and I thank You in advance for what has been produced. I decree this is the year of the harvest. Let there be more to come. I decree that as I yield myself to Your wisdom, I will bear fruit that brings You glory and honor. In Jesus' name, Amen.

Without Partiality

Wisdom does not show favorites. It is free from bias. It is not prejudiced. James gave us an example of an attitude of partiality:

> My brothers, as believers in our glorious Lord Jesus Christ, don't show favoritism. Suppose a man comes into your meeting wearing a gold ring and fine clothes, and a poor man in shabby clothes also comes in. If you show special attention to the man wearing fine clothes and say, "Here's a good seat for you," but say to the poor man, "You stand there" or "Sit on the floor by my feet," have you not discriminated among yourselves and become judges with evil thoughts?
>
> James 2:1–4

When we prefer the rich to the poor, we are partial. When we prefer people of a certain race or class, we are partial. Yet true wisdom treats all persons with the same dignity and respect.

Without Hypocrisy

Finally, wisdom is not hypocritical. It will not appear one way today and another way tomorrow. When wisdom is displayed on you, what you see is what you get. It wears no mask and has no pretense. It is genuine and real.

Wisdom will check you when you are tempted to manifest hypocritical motives. It will ensure openness and truth in your responses. It will remind you of the consequences that follow your actions, causing you to consider things carefully and decide the most plausible outcome.

I love the stuff that makes up wisdom! All the ingredients I have outlined here are desirable, and wisdom contains them all. When you acquire true wisdom, these virtues fill your life. I hope you are as convinced as I am that wisdom is therefore worth intense pursuit. Let's go for it together as we make one more decree about these virtues of wisdom in our lives!

Decree to Be without Partiality or Hypocrisy

Lord, I decree that You are great and highly exalted. I thank You that You are above all double-mindedness. Let Your power renew my mind and spirit so I can be genuine and compassionate, like You. Let every thought I have be holy. Let me be the person You called me to be, whether everyone is looking or whether no one is paying any attention to me. Lord, let me be one who is who I say I am. Let me be an example of Christ. I decree that I will not lead a double life. I will not live in secret. I decree that I will not live in shame, confusion or denial. I will walk in truth. I will not practice one thing and preach another. Let there be grace for me to be who I am. I decree that I will not be given to partiality or hypocrisy. I seal this decree with the precious blood of Jesus Christ. In Jesus' name, Amen.

Rotten or Clean Fruit?

True godly wisdom comes clean and is full of character. It is Christlike and saintlike. It is calming, comforting and inviting. We must not drift into desiring wisdom from another source, wisdom that hurts others and helps us. The proof is in the fruit. Again, James warns us what to watch out for:

If you harbor bitter envy and selfish ambition in your hearts, do not boast about it or deny the truth. Such "wisdom" does not come down from heaven but is earthly, unspiritual, of the devil. For where you have envy and selfish ambition, there you find disorder and every evil practice.

James 3:14–16

Stay away from such rotten fruit. Plenty of clean fruit is available for you to enjoy and to share when you are pursuing and manifesting true wisdom.

Now that we have established wisdom's purity, we must press forward on the journey of a lifetime—discovering what God has created us to do and doing it to our maximum potential to bear fruit. That is the road to real success. Our journey of success is what we will look at in the next chapter.

Questions for Meditation

1. As you look at the virtues of wisdom, how would you rate yourself in the character aspects of purity? On a scale of 1–10, soberly look at where you rate in the following. Are you peaceable, gentle, willing to yield, full of mercy and good fruits, without partiality or hypocrisy? Praise God for where you are at this moment, but ask Him for grace to pursue these to a greater extent. Let wisdom flow to you about how to stimulate these good things in your daily walk with God.

2. If you asked people who either work with you or minister with you if you show partiality, what would they answer? How can you improve your character in terms of how you view others?

PRACTICAL TIPS

1. If hypocrisy is one of the leading accusations made against the Church, we need to present ourselves as purely as possible to the world. Do you pursue any activities or act in any ways that could be construed as hypocritical? If so, place these before God and ask Him to help you develop excellence and purity in these areas. Be sure to find someone who can hold you accountable in these areas so that another set of eyes is looking beyond any blind spots you may have.

2. Purity is not something you can will into your life. Purity can only be produced through the Holy Spirit. You need only be a teachable student. Search Scriptures that speak about purity. Write them on cards and place them on your bedside table. Read these nightly before you sleep to remind yourself of the joy of daily growing in holiness. Let wisdom speak to you as you sleep and as you awake in the morning.

9

Wisdom's Journey of Success

> Success is not a place at which one arrives
> but rather the spirit with which one under-
> takes and continues the journey.
>
> —Alex Noble

Finances were a bit tight. As pastor of a small church, I did not make a huge salary. We had enough to make ends meet, but not much extra. A few times I thought about getting an outside job, but the ministry demanded that my time be flexible. I needed the ability to set my own schedule. Clocking in from 9 to 5 would have been tough because of the demands of the ministry. This state of things made me open to Reverend Teresa's offer.

Teresa was the owner of the public Laundromat where we used to wash our clothes. She was in her late fifties or early sixties, and she really knew her Bible. She quoted Scripture consistently and talked about the Lord frequently. After visiting with her a few times while we were waiting for our laundry, she shared with Kemi and me that she wanted to offer a lease/purchase of her business to someone. She had watched us and felt we were the couple who would take good care of the business she had given so much of her life to build. We felt honored that she would consider us to carry on her legacy. Furthermore, we could use the extra income and benefit from the flexibility of owning our own business. We were definitely interested.

We set a date with Teresa to view the business books and discuss terms of transfer and business operations. When she showed me the tally for the previous month's sales, I was impressed. I was amazed at how a few quarters put into the machines could add up to a tidy sum. If we operated the business as Teresa did, we could see a profit of $5,000 to $6,000 per month. Kemi and I were beyond excited. We borrowed money to give her a few thousand down and signed the lease. We were now the new owners of Teresa's Home-Style Laundry. We changed the name, personalized the building and set out to make a fortune.

After the first few weeks, we became a bit concerned. The traffic flow was great—people continued to patronize the Laundromat in spite of the change in ownership. But the quarters did not add up. Our accounting ledger did not see the same profit margin we had seen in the reverend's book. Instead of $5,000 to $6,000 per month, we were barely making enough to pay the business bills—much less realize any profit.

As time went on, I discovered that Reverend Teresa had lied to us. She cooked her books and falsified documents to make the business appear profitable. Not only did our actual sales confirm this fact, but someone who had worked with her previously told us what she did. We had been had!

Kemi and I did our best to make the business profitable. We cut every cost and worked from open to close. We tried to multitask during those long, fourteen- to sixteen-hour days. We attempted to parent our four young children amidst customers and dirty laundry. I even conducted counseling appointments beside the washing machines. I ended up being tied down after all—the very thing I had sought to avoid.

Things escalated when Kemi developed an allergic reaction to the cleaning chemicals and had constant trouble breathing. She could no longer work in the Laundromat with me. Now I was there by myself all day, every day. My once-vibrant prayer life dwindled to almost nothing. I was spiritually dry, physically tired and still broke. Oh yes, and in debt for the loan I had borrowed to lease the business. We tried to contact Teresa to offer her the business back. She had disappeared, changing her number and relocating. Finally, I stopped paying her lease payments—the only way we could get her to contact us. When we heard from her, we gave the business back to her and paid her the money we had withheld to get her attention.

I walked away from that experience many thousands of dollars in debt and spiritually weak. What went wrong? Why had I been unsuccessful in that venture? Something was missing—I had left wisdom far behind in the transaction. I closed my eyes and my mind to many things I normally would have heeded because I let the fact that Teresa was an older lady and a supposed reverend stand in wisdom's way.

I made the same mistake that Joshua made with Gibeon. After Joshua and the children of Israel conquered Jericho and Ai, they prepared to move on to the next city—Gibeon. The Hivites living there knew they could not defeat the Israelites, so they concocted a plan. They donned old clothes and worn sandals, and they packed moldy bread and tattered wineskins in an effort to make the Israelites think they were from a far country. The Israelites bought the story, making a covenant with them that they would not destroy them (see Joshua 9).

Everything looked so perfect. Everything seemed to check out on the surface.

I understand what was going on in Joshua's mind. As a result, I understand Joshua's mistake. Like me, in his zeal he did not listen to wisdom the way he should have. Looking back on my situation, I should have caught many signs that something was not right. But overarching everything was the way I stepped out of wisdom's lane for my life and paid a price for it.

I have learned some valuable lessons since that time. One lesson is that wisdom will *always* lead us to success, 100 percent of the time—if we let it. In this chapter, I want to define success for you and show you how true wisdom, when we yield to it, will always show us the proper path to take to realize the desired results in our lives.

Prayer to Follow Wisdom's Discernment

Father, I ask in the name of Jesus that You help me always to see wisdom's clues. Grace me to see beyond the obvious. Help me discern the intent of others' hearts, just as Jesus did, before I make decisions. Help me avoid the traps laid before me in the future. Thank You, Lord, for hearing my prayer. In Jesus' name, Amen.

What Is Success?

Before we can see how wisdom will lead us toward success, it is important that we define what success is. Many people have the wrong concept of success. I did a random street survey asking people to share in a few words what *success* means to them. Their answers represent what many think:

Answer #1—*"Success is being able to have the material things I desire."* This answer cannot be accurate because the entire book of Ecclesiastes teaches that success will not be found in things. Possessions typically provide temporary fixes. Success cannot be measured in this way.

Answer #2—*"Success is accumulating great wealth."* Ecclesiastes 5:10 finds fault with this answer. It says, "Whoever loves money never has money enough; whoever loves wealth is never satisfied with his income." The bumper sticker that says "He who dies with the most toys wins" is quite deceptive. Many have died with abundant "toys," yet they were far from successful. Material possessions do not satisfy, nor do they provide success. Oil industrialist John D. Rockefeller, the founder of Standard Oil Company, was the first billionaire in the United States. Some consider him the richest man in history if you adjust for inflation. He was once asked how much money it would take to satisfy him. His answer: "Just a little bit more." Wisdom has a better way to determine success.

Answer #3—*"Success is when you possess sincere happiness."* Defining success as happiness is rooted in self-centeredness. Additionally, happiness is a fleeting emotion. It describes your emotional state as a result of something that happens. Since no one is happy all the time, success could not possibly be defined that way. A consistent search for happiness usually results in misery. People whose only goal in life is to be happy are destined to fail at it.

Answer #4—*"Success is a sense of pride in the difference you make."* At first blush, this sounds like a noble answer. Making a difference should provide a great deal of internal satisfaction, but does it equate with success? We are getting closer to the definition of success, but making a difference is too broad a goal. Making a difference in what? Do all topics apply? A true definition of success needs to be a bit more narrowly defined.

Answer #5—*"Success is achieving my goals."* Many feel success arrives when the last item is checked off on a list of desired objectives. I have counseled people over the years who just knew they would be happy or successful once the right relationship came along. For other people it was the right job or the right car. Success cannot be pinpointed in this way because once you achieve your goal, what next? I do not know about you, but many of my goals will never give me a feeling of success. Some are just tasks that I need to complete.

Each of these randomly selected opinions represents the way many feel about success. Some of these opinions may include elements of success, but none of them define it totally.

How does wisdom view success? *Success is finding what you were created to do and working at it to your maximum potential.* Notice I said working at it to your *maximum potential*, not totally reaching it. It is important that we conceptualize success as an expedition, not a destination. Wisdom knows working toward success is a journey. Our concept of success is linear in nature, but wisdom sees success in three dimensions that have to do with our purpose, our best and our character. Make the following decree about wisdom with me; then let's look at each of these dimensions in more detail.

Decree to Align Our Hearts with God

I decree that my heart will align with God's heart concerning what is right for me. I decree that I will not climb a false ladder of success, only to realize later in life that it is leaning against the wrong building. I declare that my desires and intentions will be in line with what is right for me in God's eyes. In Jesus' name, Amen.

My Purpose

God created each of us on purpose and for a purpose. He told Jeremiah that before his birth, he had already been chosen for a purpose: "Before I formed you in the womb I knew you, before you were born I set you apart; I appointed you as a prophet to the nations" (Jeremiah 1:5). This verse fascinates me. Not only did God ordain us for a purpose in life, but He wrote His desire for all of our days in a book before we were ever born (see Psalm 139:16). If that does not prove we have a purpose, what does?

Some may feel such knowledge from God is only for preachers and prophets. Not so. God creates all of us with a clear destination in mind for us. He is ready to give us wisdom to understand what our destination is, and He also gives us the opportunity to pursue it. We must understand that we are each an intentional, custom creation. He customized us for a specific task, and He formed everything about us with that in mind. All of us have a purpose, and the first step to success is discovering what that purpose is. We could spend our lives doing everything the world says we must do to be a success and still miss the purpose for which God created us. We must find our purpose in Him and pursue it.

I have discovered that there are no cookie-cutter methods for finding one's purpose. God's children are extremely diverse, so what might work for one might not work for another. Wisdom provides tips that help all of us on that path. The pages of God's Word are full of wisdom that can help us find our specific purpose. Most Christians search for inspiration and motivation in the Bible, but few are looking for God to reveal their destiny through what is written there.

The Bible's wisdom comes first and foremost, but you also can find wisdom in other resources designed to help people assess their gifts, talents, deep desires and abilities. You will want to consider your personal history and the opportunities available to you. Taking personal inventory is helpful. Contemplate what you most enjoy doing and what experiences draw and fulfill you.

Asking these simple questions while submitting to wisdom's counsel will usher you into the specific purpose God has in mind for you. Many employers and ministries use tools such as these to advise people about pursuing a particular career path or to help them discover their unique place of ministry in the local church.

Such tools, however, cannot replace the Owner's manual—the Bible. You must apply its wisdom to each tool you use on your journey toward successfully finding the purpose for which God created you. To apply wisdom in this way, you must pray, read God's Word consistently and be open to the Holy Spirit speaking to your heart.

Prayer for Revelation of Purpose

Father, I ask that You lead me into a specific revelation of my purpose. You alone know what I am created to do. I realize You knew me before I was ever born and designed me with specificity. Although You gave me a free will, I want to do Your will. Please show me the way I should go. You know me best and can communicate with me in a way that I will comprehend. Please guide me. In Jesus' name I pray, Amen.

Doing My Best

Finding out what God wants us to do is one thing; doing it to the best of our ability is another. In the parable of the sower, Jesus taught us about production. Whenever I think of my potential, I think of this parable with its harvests of thirty, sixty and a hundredfold. Some people only amount to 30 percent of what they could be. Others amount to 60 percent. Still others—albeit very few—amount to a 100 percent, full expression of their potential.

When it comes to finding our purpose, wisdom becomes our coach, guiding us along the way. When it comes to our potential, wisdom becomes our cheerleader, encouraging us onward toward a full expression of that potential. Reaching our full potential takes diligence. Proverbs 6:6–11 sets forth the ant as an example of diligence:

> Go to the ant, you sluggard;
>   consider its ways and be wise!
> It has no commander,
>   no overseer or ruler,
> yet it stores its provisions in summer
>   and gathers its food at harvest.
>
> How long will you lie there, you sluggard?
>   When will you get up from your sleep?
> A little sleep, a little slumber,
>   a little folding of the hands to rest—
> and poverty will come on you like a bandit
>   and scarcity like an armed man.

Sluggards have natural gifts and a God-given purpose like anybody else, but because they feel entitled to more than they have earned, they accomplish very little. No matter how gifted a person is, if he or she follows the path of a sluggard, potential is stopped in its tracks. Diligence, on the other hand, creates an open channel for potential to flow through an individual. It helps us reach our best. Wisdom certainly wants us to grow to become the best we can be.

My Character

People characterized by wisdom take personal responsibility for their actions. That is one of wisdom's key principles that aids us in achieving true success. Many people attempt to soothe themselves by blaming someone else for their lot in life. I taught math for a short while and noticed that when my students did well on a test, they would say *they had made* an A or a B. When they did poorly on a test, they instead would say *I gave them* a D or an F. What a stark difference—they took credit when they did well and shifted the blame to me when they performed poorly!

Our tendency to shift blame originates with our first parent—Adam. After disobeying God by eating the forbidden fruit, he blamed Eve for his sin. Like Adam, we often make excuses for our plight in life. We blame our dysfunctional parents or our overbearing teachers. I guarantee that for any excuse we can think of, somebody somewhere faced even worse circumstances, yet overcame them. There really is no good excuse for shifting blame. Excuses are nothing but stepping-stones to failure. They place us on a downward path toward creating "blind spots" in our character. Wisdom, however, tells us to take personal responsibility for our actions. This sets us up to learn from our mistakes and avoid mishaps in the future.

I have learned that God puts a lot of stock in our individual ability. When we stand before Him in heaven, we will be judged according to our deeds in the flesh. How could God righteously judge us if we do not have personal responsibility for our actions? If we were able to blame someone else for our failures, how could we be sentenced? Both judgment and the fact that God gives us a free will testify to our personal responsibility more than anything else.

When it comes to personal responsibility, it is important not to compete with others. Scripture teaches that nobody can stop you (see Romans 8:31), but that also means nobody can *start* you. The man or woman in the mirror is ultimately responsible for what you do with yourself.

Failure also will be part of our journey, but through wisdom we can learn to benefit from it. Everyone makes mistakes. Wisdom does not let the mistakes of yesterday drown our tomorrow. Those who succeed must develop the ability to fail without quitting. Max Lucado, the bestselling Christian writer of over 75 books, was rejected by 14 publishers before one accepted him.

The only person who never failed at something is the person who never got out of the bed. When failure comes, we cannot give up. We must see the bigger picture and use it as a means for growth. If we let failure keep us down, we will never benefit from the learning experience it offers. Wisdom calls failure a learning curve. Paul failed miserably when he persecuted Christians and helped kill them. After being confronted by Christ and surrendering to Him, Paul finally learned to let go of the past and move into his full potential and purpose. He chose to grow in Christ.

Personal growth does not happen automatically—it is a choice. God desires His children to grow in many ways. We should be growing stronger in our gifts, talents and purpose. To do that, we should develop a vision for the areas in which we desire growth. We must also become teachable, realizing that we do not know everything. We are responsible to develop a plan for our growth and seek out the knowledge we need. If we will commit to continual daily improvement, it will bear fruit in our lives. Do not let the past drag you down. Remember, yesterday ended at midnight.

Wisdom Serves with Humility

Another key principle to recognize is that wisdom advocates serving with humility. Over the years, wisdom has taught me how a little pride can destroy great success. As believers, we ought not live by sheer ambition. Our assignment is to be servants, and operating as a servant requires humility.

Let me give you a picture of how positioning ourselves in humility can safeguard us. My daughter had a dream in which several people she knew, including our family, were trying to reach a certain destination. To get there, we had to crawl on our bellies under some barbed wire for quite a distance. Enemies were shooting bullets right above the wire from every direction. My daughter screamed out to us, "You have to stay low so you don't get shot!" In the same manner, we must stay low in our estimation of ourselves so that the arrows of Satan do not penetrate us. We are in danger of taking a bad fall when we are puffed up with pride.

Humility means we come before God knowing that we are dependent on Him for our very breath. Put another way, humility is wisdom's estimate of who we really are, with gratitude for God's grace toward us. Vertical humility admits that we are nothing and God is all in all. Horizontal humility is being willing to serve humanity, realizing that we are simply recipients of grace. This sets us up for a free flow of God's grace, which in turn produces success.

Be aware that many who espouse worldly principles of success actually teach the principles of pride. Some books instruct you to take advantage of other people and look out for number one—yourself. But true biblical success, wisdom's way of success, demands the opposite. We must strive to be like Jesus in humility and service.

Wisdom has led me to practice the principle of humility. I apply it in a few different ways that may help you, as they have helped me. In a disagreement, I try to defer to my opponent quickly whenever possible. I also practice social humility by deferring to others concerning places of honor and the like. For example, when I am invited to speak at a church, I do not seat myself in the pulpit area. Rather, I worship with the people in the pews. The only reason I would sit up front is if I am asked to do so. I also never insist that anyone call me by my title.

In addition, I try to serve those hired to serve me. Our church's ushers and staff members typically seek to serve me by opening doors for me, carrying my bag or other heavy items and providing whatever I need. I try not to let them outserve me, so I open doors for them, carry their bags and get them bottles of water. I do my best to stay utterly dependent before God, in a posture of service. To me, this is wisdom. To God, this is a key principle to success. To you, it can be an awesome way to live. God alone will exalt us in due time as we embrace humility.

Ultimate Success

What better way to be successful than to have God initiate the purpose for our lives, reveal this purpose to us and keep us in its path as we emulate Christlikeness? Wisdom has a great plan! I cannot think of anything in life more important than finding our God-given purpose and fulfilling it with passion. This is success—ultimate success.

Wisdom will draw you toward true success as iron draws a magnet. It will never lead you on a rabbit trail of unnecessary activity. Wisdom is about purpose. It will help you live on purpose, with purpose. It will lead you to embrace these and many other principles that will aid you in finding God's destiny for your life and fulfilling that destiny to the best of your ability.

Prayer to Maximize Moments

Father, help me make the most of every opportunity that You provide for me. Aid me in taking inventory of my life to identify activities and relationships that waste my time and rob my energy. Help me do my best with what I have. Grant me the wisdom to order my day and my life in such a way that I will achieve maximum productivity. I thank You in advance for grace in this area. In Jesus' name, Amen.

As we press in to wisdom's embrace, we need to know how to gain wisdom and maintain it. In the next and final chapter, I will discuss this in more detail. For now, let's review how to acquire more wisdom about your journey to true success.

QUESTIONS FOR MEDITATION

1. Take your own informal survey of how the people you know define success. Ask at least five co-workers, family members or acquaintances to give you a one-sentence definition. As you look at their answers, allow wisdom to show you how their lives compare to their definitions. Then examine your own thoughts about your personal success quotient. Have there been times when you had some measure of success in other people's eyes, but found yourself wanting?

2. When has wisdom tapped you on the shoulder and asked why you did not humble yourself in a situation or

with a particular person? Are there people with whom it is difficult for you to be humble? Can you think of ways to eliminate the possibility of exuding a prideful spirit around these particular people?

PRACTICAL TIPS

1. Time management is a skill we all need in order to manage our lives and prepare for success. Here are some ideas about how to increase your effectiveness in this area:
   • Set goals. If you do not know where you are going, you will never arrive.
   • Prioritize goals into the daily activities necessary to accomplish them.
   • Write down your goals. When you finish one task, it helps to know what is next.
   • Avoid time wasters. Try not to give time to unproductive activities.
   • Avoid people who regularly waste your time.
   • Evaluate your day every evening and plan to improve the next day.
   • Do not be so rigid with your plans that you cannot tolerate interruptions. Jesus was often interrupted on the way to do what the Father assigned Him.

2. What is your purpose? What has God graced you with to do His will? If you use a calendar, a planner or a to-do list, write your purpose on the top of each page for at least four weeks. Each day as your eyes catch sight of your purpose, take a moment to thank God for the privilege of that purpose and ask for His grace to help you grow in its success. Be sure to allow wisdom to speak to you each day.

10

How to Make Wisdom Your Own

> Wisdom is supreme; therefore get wisdom.
> Though it cost all you have, get under-
> standing.
>
> —Proverbs 4:7

I hope that by now your desire for wisdom has significantly increased. Writing this book has fired me up—I want more wisdom! I am determined to make it my primary pursuit, but how we get wisdom is the question of the hour. There are four biblical ways we can acquire wisdom—desiring it, asking for it, having faith and having wisdom imparted to us. Let's take a moment to discuss these.

Desiring Wisdom

If you would like to have wisdom, then you must strongly desire it. Not much comes our way without desire on our part. God does not force wisdom on us. Free will demands that before we can receive anything from God, we must desire it. Proverbs 2:1–7 (NKJV) tells us,

> My son, if you receive my words,
> And treasure my commands within you,
> So that you incline your ear to wisdom,
> And apply your heart to understanding;
> Yes, if you cry out for discernment,
> And lift up your voice for understanding,
> If you seek her as silver,
> And search for her as for hidden treasures;
> Then you will understand the fear of the LORD,
> And find the knowledge of God.
> For the LORD gives wisdom;
> From His mouth come knowledge and
>   understanding;
> He stores up sound wisdom for the upright;
> He is a shield to those who walk uprightly.

Look at the verbs in these verses: *cry* after wisdom, *lift* up your voice for understanding, *seek* her and *search* for her. These are all words and phrases that speak of strong desire. Desire is a central component of faith, and without faith, we will not get anything from God.

We must see the potential our lives would have, and we must imagine our opportunity to bring more glory to God, if we were endowed with more wisdom. We should envision the blessing that will come upon our children and the prospect of changing our family tree if we become wiser. These desires must drive us toward wisdom.

King Solomon pleased God when he asked for wisdom. From the first time I read that, wisdom is something I have desired. I want it for its amazing benefits, but I also want it because desiring it pleases God. Israel's Golden Age was a direct result of Solomon's golden gift of wisdom. It is interesting that if King Solomon had never asked for wisdom, he never would have obtained it. His desire led to asking, which led to receiving. We seldom ask for what we have no desire to receive.

What happens if your desire for wisdom is not that strong? Then come to God as you are and be honest. Say, "God, I really would like to desire wisdom. Would You please put more desire for Your wisdom into me?" This is the right place to start. If you pray sincerely, God will give you both the desire for wisdom and the ability to receive it. Pray this prayer, too:

Prayer to Stir Up a Desire for Wisdom

Heavenly Father, I thank You for wisdom's significance. I ask that You help me stir up my desire for wisdom. Though my head may understand that I need wisdom to walk in my destiny daily, I ask You to relentlessly prick my heart and jog my memory so that I will listen to wisdom every day of my life. Do not let blankets of ungodliness or the influence of a worldly rationale strangle my pursuit. Lord, I believe You hear me this very moment and have already dispatched Your angels to answer my prayer. Thank You for helping me seek wisdom. In Jesus' name, Amen.

Asking for Wisdom

The second method of acquiring wisdom involves asking for it. As I mentioned before, the apostle James teaches us, "If any of you lacks wisdom, he should ask God, who gives generously to all without finding fault, and it will be given to him" (James 1:5).

Basically, wisdom is yours and mine for the asking. The Lord has designed it this way in order that we exercise our wills, matching ours with His. We must ask, and we shall be given. We must seek, and we shall find. We must knock, and the door shall be opened to us. James 4:2 says it again: "You do not have, because you do not ask God." Asking is the pathway toward receiving the wisdom we desire.

Every example you have read in this book can become your own example in one way or another. All these stories can become your stories. The accounts of how wisdom can build our natural gifts or help us discover God's purpose for our lives can all become your reality. Wisdom is an equal-opportunity blessing. You can have it if you ask for it. All I have written thus far is meant to inspire a desire within you that results in a prayer for more wisdom.

Asking for wisdom may be simple at times—a whisper or quick prayer. But asking can also be intense—sometimes done with tears. At times, asking will be founded upon fasting. Occasionally, asking will be characterized by an inward groaning that cannot be uttered. Sometimes you may ask and receive your answer in an hour. Other times, you may not see your answer for a year. I have been asking God for certain requests for the last 23 years, and I have yet to see them answered. Yet I know I will see the answers, so I keep asking. It is wisdom to ask, trusting that God sees the end from the beginning. The promise in James 1:5 is that if we ask for wisdom, it will be given to us. We must stand on this truth and ask!

Having Faith

Third, we must have faith throughout the process of receiving wisdom. Though we may ask with intensity, we must believe tenaciously. James also warns us that we must ask in faith, without wavering.

But when you ask, you must believe and not doubt, because the one who doubts is like a wave of the sea, blown and tossed by the wind. That person should not expect to receive anything from the Lord. Such a person is double-minded and unstable in all they do.

James 1:6–7

We must not ask and then doubt—for it would prohibit us from receiving. We must ask with the faith of little children. I have two grandchildren, a boy and a girl. Whenever I promise them something, they take me at my word. They never consider that Granddad might not be able to deliver their request. This is the kind of faith James says we must have when we approach God for wisdom. If we come to God in this way, we will not be denied.

Faith is to wisdom as a key is to a door. You can still get through a door without a key. You might need to break the door down, or you might need to unscrew all the hinges and take it off its frame, though. These actions are awkward and labor intensive; all you really need is a key to unlock the door. Likewise, wisdom is unlocked most easily through faith.

Impartation

Finally, we can receive wisdom through impartation. A wisdom-filled person might lay hands on someone else and impart a portion of wisdom to him or her. Scripture gives an example: "Now Joshua son of Nun was filled with the spirit of wisdom because Moses had laid his hands on him. So the Israelites listened to him and did what the Lord had commanded Moses" (Deuteronomy 34:9).

I shared with you earlier that wisdom is a gift. Scripture makes it clear that gifts can be imparted. I recently preached a message titled "The Mantle of Wisdom" in the church I pastor. At the end of the message, I felt the Lord wanted me to lay my hands on people and impart what wisdom I had. I obeyed the Lord's leading, and God mightily honored it. People literally experienced an increase of knowing what to do in difficult situations. The next time you find somebody with a good spirit who is full of wisdom, ask him or her to lay hands on you and impart some of it to you.

Decree to Impart Wisdom

I decree that I will impart godly wisdom all of my days. I decree that I will be able to lay holy hands on people and impart to them the same wisdom God has bestowed on me. I decree that when I lay my hands on people, spiritual gifts will be imparted and established in every individual whom I touch. Lord, I believe that You will perform these things according to Your Word. In Jesus' name, Amen.

The River of Wisdom

Take a moment to review the ways in which we can receive wisdom. We must desire wisdom with all sincerity and ask for it with all earnestness. We must believe in faith that we will receive it, and if an opportunity presents itself, we must ask someone with wisdom to pray for us and release it into our lives.

Let's practice each of these four ways of gaining wisdom so that we might readily receive it. To get started, answer these last questions for meditation, and then read and pray through the wisdom Scripture I provide in the final practical tips section. That Scripture from Proverbs 8 would be good to meditate on daily as God begins unleashing the power of heavenly insight into your life by revealing the secrets of biblical wisdom.

Let's begin our journey now and see how deeply we can swim in the river of wisdom. Wisdom is too priceless and precious a gift to delay!

QUESTIONS FOR MEDITATION

1. Have you ever been placed in a position where you needed to make an extreme decision on the spot and you asked God to help you? What was the outcome of that decision? Did you believe you heard from God in making your choice?

2. List three life-changing decisions you have made without first seeking the wisdom of God. Describe the outcomes of those decisions.

PRACTICAL TIPS

In chapter 1, I suggested keeping a wisdom notebook or journal. Continue that practice even though you have reached the end of these pages. As you read God's Word, continue capturing pearls of wisdom from Scriptures such as the one that follows. Keep recording wisdom you discover in messages you hear or in talks you have with godly men and women. Apply the principles and attributes of biblical wisdom to your own life and watch how the Spirit of God transforms you.

Wisdom's Call

Does not wisdom call out?
Does not understanding raise her voice?
On the heights along the way,
    where the paths meet, she takes her stand;

beside the gates leading into the city,
at the entrances, she cries aloud:
"To you, O men, I call out;
I raise my voice to all mankind.
You who are simple, gain prudence;
you who are foolish, gain understanding.
Listen, for I have worthy things to say;
I open my lips to speak what is right.
My mouth speaks what is true,
for my lips detest wickedness.
All the words of my mouth are just;
none of them is crooked or perverse.
To the discerning all of them are right;
they are faultless to those who have knowledge.
Choose my instruction instead of silver,
knowledge rather than choice gold,
for wisdom is more precious than rubies,
and nothing you desire can compare with her."

Proverbs 8:1–11

Notes

Chapter 2: Wisdom's Playbook

1. James Strong, *Strong's Exhaustive Concordance of the Bible* (Peabody, Mass.: Hendrickson, 2007), 116.
2. Ibid.
3. David O. Oyedepo, *The Wisdom That Works* (Lagos, Nigeria: Dominion Publishing House, 2006), 7.
4. *Merriam-Webster Online*, s.v. "Wisdom," www.merriam-webster.com.
5. Strong, *Exhaustive Concordance*, 123.
6. Ibid., 58.
7. Ibid., 39.

Chapter 3: Wisdom: The Insight Whisperer

1. Paul Barker, "George Washington Carver," 2006, http://paulbarker.org/george_washington_carver.html.
2. James Strong, *Strong's Exhaustive Concordance of The Bible* (Peabody, Mass.: Hendrickson, 2007), 118.

Chapter 4: Knowledge: Wisdom's Brilliance

1. Thomas Edison, quoted in Martin André Rosanoff, "Edison in His Laboratory," *Harper's*, September 1932, http://harpers.org/archive/1932/09/0018333.

Chapter 5: Attitude: A Glass Half-Full of Wisdom

1. Napoleon Hill and W. Clement Stone, *Success through a Positive Mental Attitude* (New York: Pocket Books, 2007), 7.

2. Scott Hamilton with Ken Baker, *The Great Eight* (Nashville: Thomas Nelson, 2008), 93.

3. Frederick Langbridge, *A Cluster of Quiet Thoughts* (London: Religious Tract Society, 1900).

4. Charles Austin Miles, "In the Garden," public domain, 1913.

5. John Hagee, "Philippians 4:13 —April 6, 2012" daily devotional, John Hagee Ministries, jhm.org.

Chapter 6: Wisdom's First Commandment

1. Judson Cornwall, *Let Us Praise/Let Us Worship* (Gainsville, FL: Bridge-Logos, 2006), 39.

2. Brennan Manning, *The Furious Longing of God* (Colorado Springs: David C. Cook, 2009), 42.

Chapter 7: Wisdom's Second Commandment

1. Martin Luther King Jr., *Strength to Love* (Cleveland: Collins World, 1977), 56.

2. Philip Yancey, *Rumors of Another World* (Grand Rapids: Zondervan, 2003), 223–224.

About the Author

Kyle Searcy is a highly respected pastor, prayer warrior, teacher and author. His personal walk and public ministry are marked by uncommon fervency and passion for Jesus Christ. He believes strongly that in our relationship with Jesus Christ, deeper than just going to church, we can have passion, sincerity and purpose. Kyle demonstrates by his lifestyle that our passion for Christ can be so deep that it will possess our innermost being and become the overwhelming motivation for all we do.

Apostle Kyle, with B.S. and M.Ed. degrees in mathematics from Alabama State University, is cofounder of Fresh Anointing House of Worship in historic Montgomery, Alabama. FAHOW's vision is "E3"—to *exalt* the Lord, *extend* the Kingdom and *empower* the people. Kyle also serves as overseer of eight FAHOW churches in the United States and of Fresh Oil Fellowship of Churches International, with more than 170 churches in Africa, including Liberia, Nigeria and Ghana. He is a member of the International Apostolic Council (IAC), composed of the founding fathers of the International Communion of Evangelical Churches (ICEC) led by the first presiding bishop, Harry R. Jackson Jr.

Author or coauthor of nine books, Kyle partnered with Lou Engle in 2008 to bring The Call prayer movement to Montgomery. Kyle has appeared on Trinity Broadcasting Network (TBN) locally as a host and guest.

Kyle is married to the beautiful and anointed Kemi, a native of Ghana, West Africa, and a dynamic woman of God in her own right. Pastor Kemi complements Kyle's ministry with an international flavor, along with an uncommon passion for prayer and intimacy with Jesus. Kyle and Kemi have two daughters, Biola Searcy-Hollis and Funmi, and two sons, Paul and Christopher. They also have two grandchildren, Nathan and Abigail.

To learn more about Kyle's ministry and books, or to inquire about having him speak at your next event, please visit www.kylesearcy.com.